LIFE?

SAY YES TO LIFE

Marta Ribeiro

Order this book online at www.trafford.com
or email orders@trafford.com

Most Trafford titles are also available at major online book retailers.

Print information available on the last page.

ISBN: 978-1-4120-6037-0 (sc)

Trafford rev. 03/14/2023

www.trafford.com

North America & international
toll-free: 844-688-6899 (USA & Canada)
fax: 812 355 4082

INTRODUCTION

Today, May 5th 1990, I am trying to scribe the Introduction of the book that I propose to write.

Why did I choose this date? Because it is today my 49th Birthday and I will start the "decade of 50th", as my daddy use to say.

I felt, after many reflections, that if I propose to write a book which would be profound, it would be not only remembrances of facts, but all other facets of my life that make me, Marta, uniquely Marta. If I did just that I could say at the end "That was my story".

I am not a writer, I don't necessarily have a literary inclination, but I'll recount some of the important events of my life. You will find interesting reading, I am sure.

Visnja Gembicki first gave me the idea to write a book about my life. She is the mother of Nika and Lella; these two girls were the first baby-sitting job I had when I came to USA. They lived in Chicago; IL.Visnja encouraged me to consider such a project. Many years later (around 1992-93) Miss Larkin also quickened my ambition to really write. She gave me some good information and suggested some magazines for writers, Writer's Digest being one of these.

Around, 1999, I had one very important help with my book. Mrs. R.B., a resident at the Nursing Home where I was working, and she was interested and helps me with that Introduction I am putting in my book.

And finally at 2002 I met T. Ricci, who is helping me to correctly my English, and put my manuscript together.

When I started to write my book, I didn't have in mind any title, because I didn't know which angle I would like to present my life. I thought a title would come to me as I preceded with my writing.

I hate definition, but if some body asked: "Marta how would you define yourself?" I would without hesitation answer: "I am a person Extremely Protected by GOD, I would say it is a scandalous this protection".

When I say extremely protected by GOD, is because HE gave me one opportunity to LIVE, or better even say He gave me LIFE. Do you know why? I hope not to shock anybody (specially my family). It's because I am a result of an abortion that did not go to completion. My apologies to my mother, but I need to talk about this terrible fact.

This does not means that I was not wanted; I never feel or have felt rejected. My mother because varied circumstances was forced to take this stand, try to the abortion, because I would be the child number 6, that time they have 5 kids(and before that 2 young babies had died). They had recently moved to Rio de Janeiro and the economical and financial situation was very bad for them. So, when my mother knew she was pregnant again, she was persuaded (please don't ask me by whom) into taking some kind of injection to cause an abortion. It did not cause an abortion, but instead caused me this facial paralysis, which I have lived with since birth.

So, I am extremely protected by God, because day by day I live.

And look, today is 05/05/1990. This means I have had 17,885 days and 429,240 hours protected and guided for Him. In consequence I'm an optimistic even if I had hard time to live and I feel I am a courageous woman. I would say I had enough courage to leave my Country and my family and try to build a new life in the USA.

I would divide my book in following parts:

My Childhood and Youth (20 years)
My life at the Congregation Santa Isabel (20 years and 8 months)
My life out the Congregation in Brazil (almost 6 years)
My arrival to America- Chicago (adaptation and legalization)
Florida (the transition one) Massachusetts (where I get my retirement and finish my book)

MY CHILDHOOD AND YOUTH

I've always heard that every good writer likes to talk about her hometown, her own family. I will try following the same but I ask myself, really, do I need to do that?

Any way, I would say that at this point I feel I am some kind of nosey.

But, any way, I am CARIOCA. I was born in a poor suburb of Rio de Janeiro, named Senador Camara, near Bangu. When I say this it's because Bangu was the closest well known place, famous for its big factory (Bangu Factory). We lived in Senador Camara until 1952, when I was 11 years old.

I have a lot of memories of the house where I was born. I remember people joking with me, asking me "Marta where were you born?" and I'd point to my parents' bedroom and smile"Over there!" For me it was a wonderful glory, because my five brothers and sisters were born in another State, Minas Gerais, in a small town named Guaxupe.

I think, before I start to narrate my life, I have to situate myself in my family. Am I right?

My father was born at Rio de Janeiro State, but was raised in Rio de Janeiro City. During one of his trips, when he was a commercial traveler, he arrived in Guaxupe, at south of Minas Gerais. There he met my mother, who was the daughter of a farmer. They fell in love with each other and married after nine months. At first, they lived on one of my Grandfather's farms.

Then the children started to be born. At this point in their lives, they decided to move to Rio de Janeiro with their 5 children, but before this was possible they had more two kids: one boy and one girl, both of whom died in infancy. The girl was named Marta. My grandmother Amelia was crazy about that name and when I was born, it was given to me, too.

Always my father was a fearless man, energetic and active, always thinking of the education of his children. He decided to move back to Rio de Janeiro, a big city with much more opportunity for the education of his children.

He bought land in Senador Camara. It was a large piece of land, like a small farm. There he tried every thing: he raised chickens, cows, etc. but at the end he subdivided the land for the construction of houses. I don't really remember the time of the chickens, because I was very small.

It is me and my first Pet, named JUJU, it was around 1942/1943

I could say that I was a very quiet child. I was the youngest child for nine years until Maria da Graca was born. Then she was the youngest child, who we named "temporona." My mother loved to say that, because at her birth my mother was 40 years old.

I could say that, sometimes, even until now I suspect some people feel sorry for me. But at the same time I would say I don't have feelings of inferiority to anybody, because I'm not afraid of talking, smiling in front of anyone.

When I remember about my childhood in Senador Camara, I remember the bicycle. How I loved to ride a bike! And I really don't know how I convinced my father to give me a bike for Christmas. Before that Christmas I had learned to ride a bike. I practiced with a bicycle owned by Sr. Joaquin. He worked with my father at the time when my father was constructing the houses. They started that construction around my house, which was located in the center of my father's land.

If you ask me if I had friends, I'll tell you I remember only one. Her name was Edinir. She was the granddaughter of D.Nila, the first person to move into one of the houses constructed by my father. Edinir's house was almost in front of my house, and she and I were the same age.

Before Edinir moved over there, I always used to play with my "invisible friends." We were inseparable. Their names were Deolinda and Japonesa. I was a very little girl then. At that time, around my house there were many orange trees. I imagined that the orange trees were the houses of Deolinda and Japonesa. Another tree, farther away, but not so far, was the school. Look! You can remember the book of Jose Mauro de Vasconcelos: "Meu pe de laranja lima." But, please, any similarity is only coincidence, because the fruit of the trees of my house were not 'lima' but a kind of sweet orange. They were "pera" a lot of acid, not sweet…

Any way, every day, when it was not raining, I liked to go to school with my friends. I would "knock, knock" at each house, complaining if they were late. I remember my grandmother gave me a little suitcase with a cartoon character on it, and a little umbrella.

At this time of my life in Senador Camara I remember a lot about my Godfather's visits most weekends. Sometimes the visits were very brief, but how I love them. He had land in Campo Grande, and my house was at the road where he went. For his visits were wonderful, because I felt that he loved me a lot and took care of my health. He was a doctor (and a good one). I was always taking vitamins and supplements. I think I was not a strong kid, because always I heard my mother say that I was born after a very hard delivery, with many problems. And under first at the protection of God, I would thank my life at the work of my Godfather, who was the doctor that assisted my mother (in the house).

My godfather was a significant person in my life. I remember the first word that I learned to write was his name, Mario, and that I did not forget the accent over a.

My family, I will say that a lot of times, in my book, were a religious family. We never missed Sunday Mass, rain or shine. My father was always a friend of the priests and once he found financial stability he loved to help the Church.

I remember a lot about the festivities in the Church: the Processions that we never missed, Coronations of Our Lady at the end of May, when I used wear a long write dress and angel wings.

My first Communion, too, was a significant milestone in my life. Everything was wonderful; my dress was specially made. I had all the things that a girl could want on this day: the remembrance and a little case in my hand with those, to give to every one present. I remember the party at my house, that evening, to commemorate my First Communion and the graduation of my oldest brother Paulo from the Technical School. I was very happy, especially happy because all my family was there, even some uncles from Guaxupe. I didn't have time to put on my white long dress again. There were so many children to play with.

But, back to my childhood playmates. I remember I loved to play with my brother named Ivinho, who was 4 years older then I was. We loved to play doll's house, although it was not a real doll's house. Outside my house we made a stove with bricks and I was the cook. If the food was good (most of the time rice with potatoes) he would eat almost everything, but if the food was burned, I would have to eat it.

Another moment that I will never forget was one day when my mother needed a sewing needle from the store of Sr.Jose. I went with my brother, because we needed to cross the very busy Santa Cruz Avenue. With the change we bought some candy, called in my language "coco de rato" (coco de rat), something like a Rice Crispy Treat. And do you know what happened? We lost the needle. My brother was carrying it, but suddenly he started to shout at me: "Marta where is the needle? If you don't find I'll open your belly and take the "coco de rat!" I was so foolish and naive that I started to cry, afraid of my mother and worse afraid of my brother opening my belly!

Sometimes when we went to Sr. Jose's store, we liked to play "step in the other one's shadow." Since I was young, and perhaps more agile, I always won, stepping more in his shadow. One time I was very close to the side walk, and he tripped- me, making me fall. I almost broke my nose, and there was so much blood around, he almost got a spanking from my brother Ismail and my mother.

Another time Ivinho called me to play with a slingshot, in Portuguese, called "atiradeira", for killing birds. But we always scared the birds; we never killed any. When my father came home there was a big scene. He asked me :"Marta where are the "estilingue?" (Another name for "atiradeira"). I did not know what estilingue meant. I tried to bring anything and everything for him, because I didn't know what he was looking for. My mother whispered to me what it was and I brought it to him and he tossed everything else away. My brother was in big trouble, because I was too young to learn how to disturb the birds' life.

It is interesting that of my other brothers and sisters in Senador camara I don't have so many things to remember, or about my relationships with them. I do remember about the soccer games (peladas) at my house in the back yard on Sunday afternoons. My brothers Paulo, Ismail, Ivinho and some of their friends would be there. They loved to put me as goalkeeper, and they threw so many balls at my body that you wouldn't believe.

I remember when I was studying in the First grade with Nair Galo. At this time I wasn't able to go to a regular school because of my physical therapy appointments. Nair's house was at the other side of the railroad. Ismail, on his way to school, was supposed to bring me with him until we crossed the railroad tracks. I would always cry, almost running to keep up with him, because he said he could not be late to school.

Another early memory was when some of my brothers were studying at the Belizario School and had to have their reports cards signed each month by my father. If some grades weren't so good, my father usually threw the paper over their face. I was very young at this time. I remember the incident, but I don't remember who was involved.

I remember when Paulo was studying at the Technical Federal School. Diva and Zulmira were attending the Course of Social Work School in downtown Rio de Janeiro. Ismail was at Naval School in Angra dos Reis, and Ivinho was at an Internate School in Niteroi, of the Salesians, Santa Rosa de Lima School.

If someone asked me if I liked to study, when I was at the Preliminary School, honestly I would have said "no!" I stayed in Senador Camara until the third grade.

In1952, in 4th grade, I went to study at Instituto Menino Jesus, at Tijuca. During the week I lived at my grandmother's house. Every weekend I went home to Senador Camara. In August, we moved to our new apartment, at the building that my father made the Construction, at Tijuca.

Staying at my grandmother's house was enjoyable for me, because I had more contact with my father's family. Aunt Ivete lived on the 3rd floor, Aunt Cecy and family lived on the 2nd floor and at the end of first Floor were Aunt Isa and family. Uncle Ismar and Aunt Irenita, who were still single, lived with my grandmother. I remember I slept in the same bed with my grandmother, at the corner, and I loved it.

I have so many happy memories of that time. How I loved my teacher Professor Humberto Spencer Galvao, who had been a classmate of my Aunt Ivete. Of my friends I remember, for example, Franci Depine, whom I met again in 1979 when I was Principal at Instituto Isabel, and she come to introduce a book written by her. She was completely deaf at that time. Another friend was Luis Fernando, a handsome boy whose attention was competed for by all the girls. I met him again in 1965 when I was studying at Universidade Santa Ursula and he was finishing at the Odontology University and soon he became the Dentist of the Instituto Isabel.

Another wonderful coincidence, in 1982, was when I met D. Ieda. I was working at the time at Lar Escola Sao Judas Tadeu. D. Ieda had been the bus attendant in 1952, when I was at 4th grade at Intituto Menino Jesus. See? Our lives are like a ball of thread, not in a good shape -I would say entangled - with memories and people with which we have lived, some leaving a good mark, and others not, and from them we construct our life. Am I right?

As a child I sometimes looked like a silly girl, because I was shy when I noticed someone looking at my paralyzed face. It was like my mouth was twisted. It is difficult to get a good analysis now of me as a little girl, because when you are a child everything is so simple, even having a face like mine.

I remember that I hated the treatments that I had to have. Some of them were very painful, such as electric massage. My parents tried everything they could, which was affordable to them at that time.

When I was still living in Senador Camara, I would go 3 times a week to physiotherapy in downtown Rio de Janeiro. We would go by train, which was not very comfortable. The first appointment was near the Campo de Santana, where I enjoyed seeing the prairie dogs. I also remember appointments at Uruguaiana Street with Dr. Jorge Medeiros.

Dr Jorge was using a new treatment with a new French machine called 'Nemectron". I was making excellent progress with this therapy. I started being able to close my right eye when I was sleeping. Not being able to close it is a problem that still causes me a lot of trouble today. Even now it does not completely close, causing me dry eyes and infections.

Doctor Jorge Medeiros had a big influence on me. He was always happy and teasing me and his attitude gave me confidence in myself. Then at that time something happened which changed that treatment. My uncle Mario (my mother's brother) and my godfather, Mario Goncalves, were both doctors, very good doctors. They discussed with my parents the treatment that I was receiving. At that time the medical community didn't accept physical therapy. My uncles advised my parents that they were throwing away money by sending me for this treatment. Of course, my parents listened to them.

Then my uncle Mario found in Sao Jose do Rio Pardo, a city not far from Guaxupe, a man (not a doctor, only a masseur) and they brought me there, where I stayed in his house doing a stupid treatment for one month. I say stupid because he was doing massage over all of my body, while my problem was only on the right side of my face.

It was at that time when I first heard learned of the possible cause of my paralysis. I was lying down in bed, maybe they forgot that I was in the room. I overheard my mother asking him whether it was possible that my paralysis could be a consequence of a shot she had taken to induce abortion. I was in shock. I never, ever mentioned this to anyone. I was too shy, at that time, to ask about it.

In August 1952, precisely on the 23rd, a Thursday, my family moved to the building that my father had constructed, Building Sto.Ivo. My father was a man of great determination. Before finishing the construction in Senador Camara, he bought land where he constructed a building with 11 apartments and one for each of his 7 children. At almost the same time he bought another parcel of land, bigger than the one in Senador Camara, to start a new development of popular houses.

It was at 1953, at the 25th Anniversary of my Parents. How I miss my family…

Life? Say Yes to Life

After I finished the 4th grade, during my vacation I studied for an admission test for the Educational Institute of Rio de Janeiro. After finishing high school, students were automatically nominated to work as a teacher for the State of Rio de Janeiro. But…I failed.

The next year I started studying at another school, Immaculate Conception School, run by the Concepcionist Sisters.

Besides attending the school I had 2 teachers. They had students preparing for the same test at the Educational Institute of Rio de Janeiro. However, I failed the entrance exam again. It looked like I did not want go to that school. At that time I was tired of hearing my parents always saying"Marta, she needs to have a good job, because maybe she will never get married." And I never asked why they felt that way. Was it because of my face? Did I look terrible? But I never asked and never question them.

When I started the 5th grade I really started to enjoy studying, without thinking about going to the Educational Institute, where all my cousins were studying. It must have been because at that time, every month, they gave a Medal for the 1st and 2nd place in each class. I enjoyed that medal on my chest.

In 7th grade, however, they put me back at the school I attended in 4th grade, Instituto Menino Jesus. There I finished the Ginasial Curso in 1957, and I remember I made nice and goods friends there, too.

In 1958 I start the Curso Cientifico (high school) at Instituto Lafayette where I had a very nice time with goods friends and great classmates.

When we move to that appartment, in Tijuca, I remember my father started to talk about the Asilo Isabel, how he appreciated the work of the Nuns (Congregacao de Santa Isabel) working with the poor children at that orphanage.

One day he went to the Mass at that Chapel, made a Prayer, and received the blessing he needed. Then he made a commitment to support one poor child for one year. This was his first contact with Mother Bernadette.

At that time I remember the Craft Fair, at the end of the year. In the month of June, every Sunday they had a Folklore Party (Festa Junina) to raise money to support the orphanage. Every May they had a Virgin Mary Celebration, each day, with the Rosary. In 1957 I started to bring my youngest sister, Maria da Graca, to study and be prepared for the First Communion. And I started to experience new feelings, inside me. I was going to Mass every morning, or receiving the Communion before the Mass, then going to school, because the Asilo Isabel was very close to my school.

I remember when I was studying English at the IBEU (Institute Brazil United State). I started at the same class, then, as my Brother Ivinho. At that time I loved to study English, but I would say it was hard to speak. It was like my tongue was stuck inside my mouth. For example, one day I was downtown and I met my teacher, Mr. Obertence. He was a tall and handsome young man. He saw me and said "Hi, Marta! How are you?" I was so confused; I felt the red in my face. I wanted to say "I'm fine!" but only smiled at him.

It is interesting how the scenes repeat in your life. When I first came to America, I remember at Disney World, when we went to the McDonald's, they always the come and ask "Can I help you?" and I ask Neida "Now what do I say?"

So far I have reminisced about my life as a student. Now I need to talk about my family, and how I felt as a member.

I don't remember a lot about my older sisters and brothers during that time in Senador Camara. I, of course, remember Ivinho, 4 years older than I am, when he was studying in Niteroi for 3 years. We used to go to visit him every Sunday. I loved taking the boat to Niteroi. After that he went to the High School at Instituto Lafayete and then to Uberaba, at Engineer University in Uberaba.

Ismail went to the Navy School, first in Angra dos Reis and finished at Rio de Janeiro 1954. He graduated in 1954, and in 1955 went to travel around the world. I remember the day his ship departed. It was beautiful.

Paulo, my oldest brother, studied Industrial Chemistry at the Technical School. Then he went to work at Compania Antactica Paulista. He stayed there almost 10 years, which was unusual. At thaht time, in my country, it was more common to be fired before completing 10 years of work, before getting stability. By the time he left that job he was married. He left it to start working with my father in construction.

Diva and Zulmira, after finishing the Ginasial course, went to Social Work School. After graduating, both started working for the government of Rio de Janeiro. They worked at the Residencial Building of Pedregulho, working with small children as activities directors. I loved go there and play with the children during my vacations.

The weddings of my four oldest sisters and brothers were remarkable events in my family, because they were married 6 months in between each one.

The first was Zulmira, who married Walter Bloise, our next door neighbor, on June13th l955 . How I remember that day! My dress was made of white nylon. At my waist was a beautiful decoration in pink, my shoes were pink high-heels - my first pair of high-heeled shoes.

And after the Celebration at Church we had a party at our home, and it was on Monday, but we had a lot of friends and family.

The next wedding was Paulo's who married Celina in Guaxupe, on January 25th1956. I remember his effort to make me his Godmother at the religious ceremony. I entered with Ismail. The ceremony was in the morning at the Cathedral of Guaxupe, and the civil ceremony had been the day before, with a simple reception at the bride's house. My dress was a special one - light-green and machine-embroidered.

Next was Diva's wedding to Custodio on July 7th 1956. She got married on nearly the same Church as Zulmira. Aunt Isa made her dress, which was so beautiful. I used the same dress I wore Zulmira's wedding, but with a new ornament at my waist and a new hat.

I remember the flower bouquet that Zulmira and Diva had made with natural flowers. It had white camellias, and was made by Maria Castrioto, a good friend of the family.

In February of 1957 was Ismail's wedding with Rejane. It was held at Santa Teresinha Church, close to Copacabana Tunnel. It was a very charming ceremony. Because my brother was in the Navy, they had the Ceremony to Cross the Swords when they left the church. At that time I was feeling like a teenager, I had a red dress, with a cute hat, too.

The wedding of my two other siblings, Ivinho and Maria da Graca, happened when I was at the

Congregation, and so I did not go to either of them.

Ivinho's wedding with Elba was on April 20, 1963 in Uberaba. I couldn't go because at that time I was at the Novitiate.

Maria da Graca's wedding with Luiz Carlos was on January 31st 1976. It was at one very difficult time for me, because the Congregation was having a Great Meeting of actualization, and I couldn't go to my parents house before the ceremony. I went there only the day before the wedding. They were married in the Church of Sacred Heart at Tijuca.

As I said before, the weddings of my four oldest siblings happened every 6 months over the space of two years. Soon after, my nieces and nephews started to be born every six months, especially the first three: Janete, Zulmira's daugther, Paulo (Paulinho), Paulos's son and Marcelo, Diva's son.

It was very exciting for me to be an aunt, because I was almost 15 when Janete was born. When I went to the Convent they were so important to me. I used to talk in my sleep, and in the Noviciate I always spoke with them: "PAULINHO, MARCELO, MARCOS! THE WINDOW IS OPEN, JUMP IN!" The next day everyone would laugh over this.

By April of 1961, I had 8 nieces and nephews, and one godson, Marcos, Diva's son. On April 28, 1961, my goddaughter Maria Matilde, Paulo's daughter, was born.

My life had been very quiet up to the time I entered the Convent. Most of my time was spent studying. I remember after I moved to Tijuca I had only a few girlfriends who lived on the same street: Amalia, Ana Maria Zamith and Silvia. Every Sunday we'd go to the Cinema at Pr. Saens Pena, at 2 pm.

I was never interested in having a boyfriend. I think I was too shy, close-minded, and maybe ashamed of my paralyzed face. Dancing? I can count how many times I went dancing. Carnaval? Only in Guaxupe at the local club with all my family around. Then? I never had a chance or maybe it's better to say I never looked for a boyfriend. I was 17 years old when I started to get the idea to go to the Convent, to be a Nun.

I can say I always thought I had vocation and really if I lived at one Convent for so long a time, I must have had that vocation, right?

But it's possible that it was also one answer that I found for my parents' uncertain feelings about my future. I was tired of hearing them say (especially my father) that Marta would have to go to the Educational Institute of Rio de Janeiro, she must have a good job because she must not get married.

I don't want to put responsibility for my decision to go to the Convent on my father's shoulders. No. It was my decision. I was never influenced by my father to do that.

I would never say that because in my way of thinking about Life, Life is constructed, day by day, by our acts and decisions. It doesn't make sense to cry over something you did or never did, because here, in this world that you have (difficult time or not) it is you who live. And better when you have a vision of God in your life, that you live life inside the God's Plan for you.

Perhaps I will still need to come back and write more about that stage in my life, my first twenty years. When I completed 20 years old I was in the convent.

I think what I already wrote should give you an idea about me, my formation inside a Catholic Family, a "typical Catholic Family." We never missed a Sunday Mass, and I grew up under a very big fear of God, but would it be better if I had had a better vision of love of God? I hope I am not saying foolish words.

MY LIFE AT THE CONGREGATION OF S. ISABEL

Now I am going to write about my feelings: What was the real reason I left my life at the Convent? And at the same time I need to think again about the real goal which brought me to live for such a long time inside the Convent.

When I was talking about my youth and my father's enthusiasm about the work of the sisters at the Asilo Isabel, I think the same feelings I was assuming by osmosis. Do I need to explain about osmosis? It is a kind of feeding of some single-celled animals and vegetables, when the animals or plants has this gradual process of assimilation or absorption . Am I right? It is a beautiful process of the single-cells lives.

I can repeat that I never, ever had in my mind the idea that one day I would get married, but I never was a child or a teenager with feelings of frustration or inferiority. Only I never took a smiling picture.... And it was my decision to go to the Convent, and I never could say that only the enthusiasm of my father made my decision to get into that Congregation. Because the work with the poor children made my goal to get into that Congregation, because I was thinking I would be CLOSER TO GOD.

I remember when I first spoke with a priest about this. He was not enthusiastic about that idea. He said to me "Marta, anywhere you are you can be close to God." And after that I was talking with Mother Bernadette, about what this priest said to me (he was at the same Parish and she knew him). She gave me the name of another priest who would direct me spiritually about my decision to be a nun, and really he was happy and enthusiastic about that.

But before that, in the middle of 1959, I heard of one Congregation, a new Foundation, and OUR LADY OF BELEM. They were only 6 nuns. I remember when I went to one Retreat, in November. I went to confession with the Cardinal of Rio de Janeiro, D.Jayme Camara. When I told him my intention to enter the Convent, how he was happy and encouraged me to do that. He said it was clear and he could see it was written with capital letters - it was what God wanted for me. Especially, he said, because I inherited an excellent religious life from my family; for example, I never had a boy friend and no sexual experience. This was the KEY, he said to me.

After that I spoke with Mother Bernadette, but at that time I was not sure which Congregation to enter. Then I decided go and talk with Sr. Sylvia Vilac, at Congregation of Missionary of Jesus Christ. It was in Santa Teresa, where the Noviciate was. After that appointment I decided to enter at Congregation of S. Isabel, in 1960. I still remember the Blessing of the Guaxupe Cathedral, when my father received the honor of comendator of the Church, because he donated the altar of the Cathedral. Then he invited two of his good friends, Mother Benadette and Fr. Miguel Lanzani (Dominican), for that festivity, and at that time my parents knew about my decision to be a Nun and go to the Convent.

Then in Guaxupe a very bad incident occurred, very uncomfortable for me. Mother Bernadette asked my mother, if they (my parents) tried plastic surgery on my face. My father was extremely upset and angry, for him this simple question was an incredible indiscretion. Then he tried to convince me not to enter that Congregation, because he was afraid that later something worse could happen to me.

But now that I really analyze that situation, I find that question really without sense. Listen: I have one side of my face paralised, they accept me or do not accept me, because what I have in my face never made difficult my life or the work I did. Then after a while, this misunderstanding quieted down, and my parents were very happy and enthusiastic about my decision to be a nun.

In Guaxupe my family was so happy because I had a very religious family, and I would be the first nun in the family. I remember that around one month before I enter the Convent. Around one month before that, I went with my father in Guaxupe to say goodbye to them, and it was very interesting. We went by bus to S. Paulo and from S. Paulo to Guaxupe by train (night train of Mogiana). In Sao Paulo we went to St. Efigenia Church. It was March,19, 1961 and this day, 35 years ago, had been my father's First Communion at the same Church where we were for the Mass. My father always loved talking about his life, his dedication to the Church. And when he was 25th years old his faith growing in his life and now I am trying write about my life.

The first person with whom I communicated at the Congregation S.Isabel was Mother Bernadette, assistant of the General Mother, Mother Divino Salvador, who was a very sick person. In 1960, the year before I entered the Congregation, I was studying at Instituto Lafayette, finishing High school, and a friend mine, Leonor, was preparing to enter another Congregation, Carmelite of Divine Providence. We talked a lot about our feelings and things that were happening before we entered the Religious Life.

I remember about the trousseau that we needed to bring. My parents decided to buy all the material, and everything would be done there and I would bring with me only others things, such as bed linen, and other personal items.

Life? Say Yes to Life

And the day I went to try on my Postulante's dress with Mother Felicidade, she was the Mother Mistress of the Noviciate; I felt a divergence between her and Mother Bernadette (the assistant) about the Documentation I was supposed to bring. It was about a letter of recommendation from my Spiritual director. The Priest didn't want to give that to me because he was my Confessor too, and it would not be correct. Mother Bernadette said it was OK, but Mother Felicidade said NO, I must bring that letter. Then? Mother Bernadette won and accepted me without the letter. It looks like nothing, yes? But later I had found a lot more diversity (opinion, maybe personal) between the Mistress of the Novitiate and the Mother assistant of the General Mother.

After that, other incidents happened about the day I would move from my house to the Convent. It was more or less decided it would be on April 20th.

Mother Felicidade decided it would be April 1st. My father was very upset: Why the rush? What was the reason? Finally, Mother Bernadette decided I would go April 20th.

That day my mother made a nice lunch for me and my sisters and brothers and their children, for me to say goodbye to them. My baggage was sent before me; I had only my pocketbook and myself. It was funny, because it was like a great feeling of separation for me, not crying, nothing.

Then? On that day April 20th, 1961, I started the time of Aspirant. It was like the first stage of preparation for the Postulate. There were 4 ladies before me and after me two more arrived. The seven of us were initiated into the Postulante on May 21st.

The aspirants were living in one attic, outside the Noviciate, and it was such a strange place, only one bathroom. But for me it was everything new and we started to be prepared to make the Poverty vows.... then? I was not scared.

I continue my study at S. Ursula University; because I had started the 1st year of the Natural History Course (my Father was still paying the University and giving me money for the transportation too).

It was a different situation for me, because I went out every morning in secular clothing. If I used the Postulante dress, I couldn't go myself, I would need company to go out.

On April 28th, Maria Matilde, my brother Paulo's daughter, was born. I was invited to be her Godmother. Then on May 20th, the day before I started the Postulate, I went to get Maria Matilde baptized, with my brother Ivinho.

On May 21st was the Ceremony when we received the Postulante dress, and it was a beautiful Ceremony. It was the Feast of the Holy Ghost, and we were 7, they said we were like the seven Gifts of the Holy Ghost. The Mass was at 9.00 am, and almost all my family was there.

I would say my first year at the University was the worse year of study in my life. I was in the time of adaptation in the Postulante life, and every morning I needed to receive Communion before Mass, have a coffee and run. At 8.00 I had to be in Class, which was in Botafogo. You know the first year at College is hard for everyone, and I had the time for adaptation at my Postulante life at the same time. But, I really made right this first year at College. I had to stop my study for 2 years, because during my time as a Noviciate, I couldn't go to school

About the Postulante time, everything was new for me. We were 18, between Postulantes and Novices, and I remember, for example, after lunch and dinner we had recreation, and played games: QUEIMADA, in my language when 2 teams need to hit the ball to the other one. I hated that ever since I was a little girl, but at that time we must play. I remember that sometimes we were treated like children. But? We needed to keep going that way, showing that we were HAPPY.

We had to work planting vegetables. This was responsibility of the Novitiate, to plant, and so on, to water, and from that garden they took a lot of

Vegetables for the Orphanage, Asilo Isabel. I loved having contact with nature, of course.

The Noviciate started November 21st, because it was a feast day of the Congregation. I was still in final exams at the College, so they postponed my entrance to the Noviciate. Instead, it would be on Christmas Eve, and the others took the Habit on November 21st.

It was great, that I received the Habit at the Midnight Mass on Christmas Eve. I used the wedding dress of my sister-in-law Celina and the veil was from my cousin Maria Augusta. It was a beautiful but simple ceremony. Then I started the Noviciate Canonic. That first year we couldn't leave the Convent, only under special circumstances. It was like a time of Spiritual preparation for the Religious Life, starting to know the meaning of each vow, and the history of the Congregation.

During the second year the Novices could go to work and sometimes live at other houses of the Congregation. That's where you learn about the work you are supposed to do, and if you accept it or not.

This first year we had classes of Bible and Liturgy, and we need to do all the work of cleaning and maintaining the Noviciate in a good condition. It was a very big place. And it was very funny because I did not know how to do anything about anything, because my mother never, ever let me do anything like that at home.

Then during the first week of the Noviciate they put me to clean the white marble stairs from the second to the third floor and the BATHROOM (and it was big one).

My Lord I made so many noise, that the others Novices were sorry for me And come to help me, because I did not know where to start, and I could say I learn the lesson,.

Other big dilemma was that I need to use a white Habit, it was long, and with one gimpy starched. And it was hard for me to keep me clean all the week, because we can change them only twice a week, it is no kidding we could change only on Thursday and Sunday the Habit and the gimpy. And sometimes, the Mistress of Noviciate was saying she would put a bib on me, believe? I was always in Panic.

I remember still so many parties we had at the Noviciate, where we sing, to recite Poems, dance, and I remember at tat I knew how to play accordion, and I was easy to make people laugh.

In 1963 at my 2nd year of the Noviciate I start to be a Teacher at one 2nd grade of the Preliminary School.

My Lord, I never had been prepared to be a teacher, but I had finished the High school, and we can apply for my Teacher Registry.

The day before the class start, only they gave the books to be followed and the list of 50 children. I was horrible scary and said It was impossible, then they divided the class and other girl, she was a Aspirant to be a Novice who had finish the High School too. We work together, prepared the class, and each one had one class of 25 children. And we had successful result at the end of the year, and I can tell I like the experience I had to be a teacher.

The date were supposed to be the Ceremony of the Vows – The Religious Professed Life, November/ 21st, was change(at that time they start to change a lot things at the Congregation), it will be on January/ 02nd, then they would have 2 special dates Jan/02nd and July/02nd (the celebration of S.Isabel).

And I was feeling so happy with the life inside the Convent.

We were 7 when we start the Noviciate, and at that time 2, of them gave up, went home, 2 were not approve by the General Counsel. Every Congregation had with the Mother General and 6 more nuns, the General Counsel, and they decided about every step in the Congregation. Then we were 4, 3 of us enter together the Noviciate and another, who 6 months before had been not approved.

I remember it was a beautiful Ceremony. The new Chapel of the Asilo Isabel was not completely finished but the Mass was there, it was the first Ceremony at that New Chapel. At that time we use to have a Godmother at the

Ceremony and I invited my Cousin Maria Augusta, and she was so happy with my invitation, and come from Guaxupe for that Ceremony.

At that time I was transferred to live at other school in Andarai, other suburb of Rio de Janeiro, it was other Orphanage, Holy Family Institute, who attend the poor children.

I remember I start again going back to study at Santa Ursula University, I was at my second year, it was 1964, and it was not a easy time at my Religious Life. I say that because in 1964 was the year of the Military revolution in my Country and I remember I was at the Class. And the Guanabara Palace(The Governor Residence) was almost next door of the University. Then at 10.00 am they cancelled all the classes and sent everybody home. I took a hide with one friend mine, and instead of going in front of the Guanabara Palace, we went through Downtown, and the Army took the streets, we were scary to death, but we get home safely.

At that time starting a lot of public manifestation, I would say

Communist. They closed the UNE (Nacional Union of students), for example, and I remember I made a Comment in my Community, about that. I said the UNE, itself, was a great deal for students (in general) and it would be a great thing for the students, and I remember I said: "Unfortunatly the Communist Party was affiliated, or infiltrate the UNE, and it was closed."

Do you believe what happening? What I said about the UNE was brought to the General Counsel of the Congregation, and? They decided I should stop going to the Class at the University. It was like a punishment, because I had Communist ideas in my head.

And at that time I start feel a big divergence in the Congregation, it was like it was divided in two blocks. I would talk later about that.

Nobody understood why I had to stop my studying at the middle of the year. My colleagues want help me, they would get me all the class, the material, they ask the permission of the Director there, I would go only for the tests, but I really couldn't do that, and I said that my reason to stop is because they need me to be a teacher at the Preliminary school.

And really I start again to teach at the Second grade, and be responsible for the discipline at the Orphanage, it was around 90 girls.

But it was no easy to take care of the discipline at that school, because it was a very old building, seems it was adapted to be a school, and a Internate School.

At the second floor it was the 3 Dormitory (Bed room), and the disposition was like they have one connection in the middle of the 3 and only one Nun was there at the time to wake up the children, and the showers were located at the basement, and the little ones, when they wet the bed, need to have a shower in the morning. Sure we had the help of some older girls, some teenagers.

But I stayed at that school only one year, 1964. At the end of the of the Recollection time, I knew I would go back (be transferred) to the Asilo Isabel, and there I lived from 1965 to 1968.

Then I start again my studying at the University, and need do again the second year. And during the next 3 years I was not a teacher at the Preliminary school, because I was having some classes in the evening (laboratory).Then I had to help at the discipline of the children, because after the Class, they have time to do their home work. And after that, with the children I have to clean the classrooms. Because the children at the Orphanage need to learn all the chores, like clean, cook, everything. It was nice and with one Nun, they help us the maintenance of the school.

In 1967 I had the idea to start the first Library at the Asilo Isabel.

It was an Infant Youthful Library, named Monsignor Amador, and that named was suggested by the children.

At that time I had two very good friends. One was Sister Teresa Fernandes, who had finished the Librarian Course. The other was Emy Pamplona, who was Director of the Library from the Educational Ministery of Rio de Janeiro. Both helped me to create the Library, and I can say it was a wonderful job. I remember I started to edit a small bi-weekly Journal about the children, with news and jokes. We sold it to the children and their families on the weekend, when they would go to spend the weekend with the family (some of them). With the money I could buy a lot of good books, collections, magazines, and I left a great number of books.

In the same year, 1967, another fate I would say very great for me, was that I helped with planning the Party of the Feast of the 40th Anniversary of the Foundation of the Congregation. It had one religious part, a special Mass offered by the Cardinal of Rio de Janeiro, and one Sport Demonstration by the children of the School. It was a gymnastics demonstration. Another teacher and I did a great job organizing, including a Parade with 8 girls doing acrobatics, some rhythmic dances, and 2 girls running across an Arc of flame.

I had a lot of problems to deal with before the event, because some old Nuns (square mentality) were upset and angry about the way some of the girls who were doing that acrobatics (Balize) were dressed. The costumes showed the form of their bodies, but they were young ones, and it was not without decency. But the other teacher helped me to make capes to cover the costumes.

In December of 1967, I finally finished my Natural History Course. I decided not go to the Graduation Ceremony because it would be at the Municipal Theatre of Rio de Janeiro, which was very elegant, and everybody would be formally dressed. Nobody cared or asked me why I wouldn't go. I made my Graduation at the Secretary of the University; it was simple, and of course I was by myself.

Life? Say Yes to Life

In 1968, I was working as discipline director of the Internate (they were 230 girls) and I took care of the section of the Older ones (they were 50), and I was teaching at the 4th grade of the Elementary School. At that time Mother Bernadette was elected Mother General of the Congregation and Sr. Deliria was her Assistant and the Superior of the Community, and she made me her Secretary.

It was a lot work, but I liked what I was doing, being involved with the children. I remember I organized a competition (Marathon) among the 3 local schools, and it was great for the kids and for me.

But at the end of the year, Mother Bernadette came to me and said I would be transferred to Uberaba, to work at SUPAM (Uberabense Society in Protection of Minors) where I would start a new middle school (Ginasio - the level after elementary school), from 5th to 8th grade, and I would be the Principal.

Think with me: I had finished the University, never had been a teacher of those grades (5th to 8th) and now they asked me to open the first School of the Congregation for those grades, and be Principal? And? Of course Marta said yes, without any question or discussion.

I can tell you it was not an easy time in my life. My father had had a bad heart attack in December 1968, and stayed at the Hospital for more than one month. He couldn't go to the Ceremony of my Perpetual Vows.

My first vows were in January 1964, renewed after 3 years and now, after 5 years, in January1969 were the perpetual vows. We were the same group of four who made together the First vows. It was a very nice Ceremony, but for me it was not the same, because my parents were not there, because my father was still in the Hospital.

He had his first Heart attack on December 14 and was admitted to the Hospital. The next day he had 3 heart failures, and then I stayed over night at the Hospital with my mother and 2 brothers, Paulo and Ivinho. The next day, Sunday, 3 of my uncles arrived, my mother's brothers from Guaxupe.

And at night, Paulo, my brother decided he would go to bring his wife and children to his home, in Campo Grande, around one hour away, to come to the Hospital to stay with my mother.

On his way back from the Hospital, he was alone in the car (my father's Kombi), and had a terrible car accident. He lost the control of the car; it was as if he lost his consciousness. He was taken to Getulio Vargas Hospital, where he had to have surgery for internal bleeding. They needed to take part of the intestine away. My father couldn't know about Paulo's car accident because of his own health situation. He missed Paulo and we told him Paulo was with mumps and couldn't come to visit him.

You can see it was not an easy situation for me. I traveled to Uberaba on January 23rd, leaving my daddy at the Hospital and my brother still in recuperation from the surgery and with one broken leg.

I traveled with one other nun, Sister Jacinta, who was going to live in another town close to Uberaba. I knew that in Uberaba I would be not only the Principal of that new School; they asked me to be the person in contact with the President of SUPAM. SUPAM was the Provider Corporation, the owner of that Orphanage. They cared for approximately 50 girls, all in need, most of them Orphans or unable to live with their families for many other reasons.

That School was under construction with financial help sent by the Federal and State Governments and the Uberaba Community. Dona Chiquinha (Mrs. Wenceslau), the President of the SUPAM, lived in Brasília. She and her husband founded that institution, because he was a Judge of the Minor, and felt the necessity of a place for abandoned girls.

The Congregation of S.Isabel was invited to live and work there. Uberaba, they received like a donation, it didn't belong to them. My work was to be like a secretary to Mrs.Wenceslau. I needed to provide for her any documentation she needs to apply for the money from the Government. After that we needed to prove it was used correctly. There was only one minor problem, which was to develop the system for what she asks and send to her. I lived there for four years and I would say I enjoyed it.

About the foundation of the new school, Ginasio Monsenhor Amador, it was made gradually, it was a night school for the girls at the Orphanage and other poor children, most of them were maiden during the day. We started with one class 1st grade (I would say comparable to 5th grade) with 40 students, all girls, and with 3 teachers and me.

I got my Certification to be a Principal. For 2 years and I did not have a Secretary, I had to do all the work and had only one person who signed. Year after the year the school grew, and finally I got a secretary; Sr. Isabel came to help me. In 1972 we had 6 classes at night and some classes in the morning, and had the first Graduation for the 8th grade.

We made a great ceremony for that 1st Graduation, it was December 8th at the Cathedral, with a Mass offered by the Bishop of Uberaba. After the Mass the Certificates were given for the students. I invited instead of one Commitment Speaker, I invited Mrs.Wenceslau and Mother Bernadette. I wanted to make a link between the SUPAM and the Congregation who ran the Orphanage and school.

At that time I remember the parades I coordinated for Independence Day and for the Spring Games. I was extremely happy with all the events for the children. We started a small band. At each Parade we had Allegoric Cars. In 1972, it was so beautiful; we made a car in the form of the Brazilian Flag.

I was in Uberaba when I started learning to drive a car. It was September 1969, I remember, because my father gave the Congregation a Kombi, and how this car helped me at my work! In Uberaba, every place I need to go was far away, and it was not a flat city, it was full of elevations. Uberaba was known as "City of Seven Mountain."

I can say that time by time I was feeling the instability in the Congregation, and its working places.

In December of 1972, Mother Bernadette was re-elected Mother General, and I was elected a Council member, though I remained in Uberaba.

Unfortunately, in February1973 Mother Bernadette died in a car accident,. She had been thrown from the car. It was a real shock for everyone and the entire Congregation. She was a very special person and had great charisma.

About one month and a half later, the Congregation left the work at the SUPAM. The Congregation had worked there for around 13 years, and it was hard work. I can tell you that leaving Uberaba didn't make sense to me at all, and leaving made a big scar inside of me.

After Mother Bernadette's death we had another election, and Mother Felicidade, who was my Noviciate Mistress, was elected Mother General. I continued on the Council.

Then I was sent back to Rio de Janeiro, to Instituto Isabel (previously Asilo Isabel). There I assumed the direction of the school, because the Principal had had surgery and couldn't stay in that position. That year, the School started the Educational Reform and start the 5th to 8th grade classes (Ginasio) and by that time I benefited from the experience from my time in Uberaba.

I was really doing a good job, working in great harmony with the teachers. They start to admit boys to the School, and gradually the number of girls at the Internate was getting smaller. They started the semi-internate and regular School, in which the children came only for classes.

In 1973 the School bought a Kindergarten, named JOANINHA (Little Lady Bug), because at that time we didn't have pre-school classes at the Instituto Isabel. When I say bought, I mean we bought the Registry and all the Educational Material. The teachers were hired by the Instituto Isabel.

It was another great experience for me. I remember a teacher of the Alphabetization Class, by the name of Arilma. In her class there was a girl, at the Internate, who went home every weekend. One Friday the brother of that little girl came for his sister. I said go and talk with Arilma, her teacher. Guess what happened? The brother of that little girl and the teacher fell in love and got married some months later. Some time before I come to America I went to visit them in Grajau, and they had already had 3 children, and were very happy.

Almost in the middle of 1974, I knew I was going to be transferred again. This time to North of Minas Gerais, in a very small city, very poor neighborhood. I was so enthusiastic with that idea, because my work would change completely, it would be more spiritual. In this city named CAPITAO ENEAS, where no priest lived, the Nuns would do the Spiritual animation, for example doing Sunday's Celebration, and distributing the Communion.

Only two nuns moved there, at that time, Sr. Perpetua and me. We lived in a house rented by the Diocese. The community gave the furniture and everything we needed. It looked like a doll's house, but very simple.

I had to work at the local school, teaching Science and Religion classes. Sr. Perpetua taught Crafts and Sewing at the local townhouse. With the money we earned we could maintain ourselves.

Every Sunday we made the Celebration and every other month a priest came, celebrated the Mass and attended the Confession. We kept the Sacrament at the Chapel in our house. We supervised the Religious class at the two Elementary Schools of the city.

I remember during Holy week we performed almost all the Ceremonies, such as the Procession and Adoration of the Cross. I can tell you I was so happy and realized this was because we could spread the Truth and help the people to discover God in their lives.

In the middle of the year, a 3rd Nun was sent to live with us at the Capital Eneas. Around October I knew I would be transferred again to Rio de Janeiro, because now they needed a Mistress of the Novitiate, can you believe it?

Remember when they needed to open a new school, they sent me to Uberaba, unprepared. Now they needed a Noviciate Mistress and they sent me for that, again without being prepared. It was unbelievable. How to improve that?

That year, 1975, was not easy for me. First because the City of Capitao Eneas was very far from Rio de Janeiro, 20 hours by bus, and we needed to take get 3 buses. I had to travel back and forth more than 3 times, because I was a Council member, for the General Council Reunion. In that city we had only one public phone.

That year my brother Paulo died, after a long illness, which began in December 1968. It was a hard time for me. I came back to Rio de Janeiro, on the night he died, and needed to come back before the Mass of the 7th day. My father could not understand that.

Then, in December 1975, I returned back to Rio de Janeiro. At that time the Congregation had am Actualization Reunion. Many things were changed, such as the name of the Congregation. It was now known as CONGREGATION OF OUR LADY OF VISITATION, instead of Santa Isabel. The Nuns could wear secular clothes, not habits, if they wanted. The Nuns could use their own name. But what happened was that the innovations created tension, because they were done without enough preparation.

At the same time the Mother General decided to separated the house of Noviciate from the Mother House. The Mother House was Instituto Isabel (previously Asilo Isabel), where the foundation of the Congregation started. Then they bought a house at Governor' Island where I moved with 3 Postulants and one old Nun.

I tell you sincerely I tried hard to adjust to that new position. To be a teacher or a Principal of a school is something you read, you learn, we have books, and so on, but how to improve a Mistress of Noviciate?

At the same time I had to teach Science in 2 schools, in the morning at Instituto Isabel, where I went by bus or car, and at night at another school in the neighborhood. With the money I received I could help to maintain the Noviciate.

I made with the 3 Postulants a very comfortable good relationship.

In 1976 I was there trying hard to do my job as Mistress of Noviciate and teacher.

But at the end of this year the Congregation had trouble in another school, Instituto Sao Jose in Jacarepagua, a suburb of Rio de Janeiro. The Mother Superior was leaving the Congregation, and the Kindergarten was without a Principal for about 5 months.

They decided to move the Noviciate to that house in Jacarepagua, and I would be the Superior of the Community, the Principal of the Kindergarten (Cebolinha was the name of that Kindergarten) and still the Mistress of the Noviciate.

At that time I had to come back to school, and do an extension of my degree, doing the Pedagogy with School Administration, because I needed that to have my Principal Certification in the state of the Rio de Janeiro. Prior to this I had only at Minas Gerais State.

Then I moved to the new School in Jacarepagua, and stayed there for 2 years. The 3 Postulants started the Noviciate and 3 more new Postulants joined us.

In the middle of 1977, the Congregation decided to construction a new house on the same land, in Jacarepagua, which would be the Residence of the General council, because the house in Governor's Island was sold.

Life? Say Yes to Life

I can say it was a very good time I had with the Novices and Postulants. We had a lot of picnics, and day trips to many tourist places and beaches. All the girls were from other states so I helped them to admire my Rio de Janeiro.

In December 1978, there was an Election in the Congregation and Mother Felicidade was re-elected for her 2nd mandate, I was re-elected too, and now became Assistant of the Mother General.

I was transferred again to Instituto Isabel. They decided to remove me as Mistress of Noviciate, because they needed me to be the Principal of Instituto Isabel. They needed me there to reorganize the 2nd grade, or High School. It was not conforming to requirements of the Educational Secretary in Rio de Janeiro.

The situation was getting extremely tense inside the Congregation. I don't want to discuss that, I want only locate me in that situation.

In 1979, while I was at Instituto Isabel, every weekend I had to go to Jacarepagua, where Mother General was living. I was her assistant and would live there too.

And now another big Novel begins.

In 1979, a group of 5 of us nuns were very dissatisfied, not with the Religious Life, but with Religious Life inside that Congregation. It became a dream for us, the possibility of founding a New Congregation. I believed it was possible and reasonable for us.

We started to talk every weekend, to discuss our future, where we would go, which Bishop could get us the support and approval. Sure I can't tell some details, because it wouldn't be ethical for me to do that. But I can say we were knocking at the door of some Bishops. The first one was in Ilheus, Bahia, another one was in Theofilo Otonni, Minas Gerais, and after that in Uruacu, Goias. Then t we went to Goias.

Before continuing I need talk about July 1979. I said before I was really enthusiastic with the idea of starting a new Congregation. My life became so turbulent over that. And the crisis? It was worse because in a Congregation when the Mother General and four Nuns intended to leave, and 3 of them were Council members - it was like a disaster, yes?

I remember on July 13 my father was admitted to the Hospital and I couldn't drive him, or go to visit him at that day, because I was so busy. I went only twice to see him at the Hospital, once the next day when he received the Last Sacrament, and on Monday morning for a couple of minutes.

On Tuesday, the Mother General had an audience with the Cardinal of Rio de Janeiro, and I had to go with her. At the audience she was communicating with the Cardinal about her and 4 other Nuns leaving the Congregation at the end of the year. After that we went straight to Jacarepagua, for a Council meeting.

The next day when I came back to the Instituto Isabel, I saw the Hospital building and my heart was broken, because my father was there, and I did not have time to go there to see him. They did not give me an opportunity for that, and he died that night. They woke me up around 1.00 a.m. with that news, because the telephone was not working in the Convent. (Crisis? Yes it was, it was not due to a financial problem, I am sure about that). I went to the Hospital with another Nun, and stayed with my mother and relatives.

During the day time, I had to go to a Community Meeting at the Instituto Isabel, and came back almost at the time of the Funeral. After his 7th day Mass at the Chapel of the Instituto Isabel, I had to travel to Petropolis with the Mother General and another Nun to meet the Bishop of Ilheus. I couldn't stay at my mother's side with my family and go with them to the Cemetery, as was the custom at the end of the 7th day Mass. It was awfully difficult for me, but at the time I really considered it normal, the way they would treat me.

After the meeting in Petropolis with the Bishop, Mother Felicidade and I went to Ilheus, and stayed there for 2 days. It did not go well, and we decided to find another Bishop. Then I went with another sister to Teofilo Otoni, MG to talk with that other Bishop. He was very polite, but again no good result for the new Congregation. Finally the Bishop of Uruacu, Goias accepted us.

In January 1980, we went to Uruacu. We were 5 sisters. We went to live at a House where the Diocese used to hold meetings. It was called TRAINING HOUSE OF THE DIOCESE, and they put as Coordinators of the House.

As soon as we were there the Bishop gave up helping us. To start the new Congregation, he was thinking to open a Secular Institute, not a Congregation. He was really in need of sisters to work at that Training House. Then he introduced us to an Auxiliary Bishop in Brasilia, because that Bishop was going to move to Novo Hamburgo, at Rio Grande do Sul, where a new Diocese was being created.

At that time, 2 of the other Nuns and I decided not go to Novo Hamburgo and start this new Congregation. We felt it would be the same as the life we had at the Congregation. One who gave up going to that new Foundation went to a monastery in Sao Paulo, and the other one planned to come back to the same Congregation at the end of the year. When we finished our one year we would ask permission to be let out.

In May 1980 Mother Felicidade went to Novo Hamburgo, one sister went to the Monastery, and 3 of us stayed in Uruacu, because we made the agreement to coordinate the Training House for one year.

Of course Mother Felicidade had with her going to Novo Hamburgo 3 more Nuns who left the Convent. Everything after that, about my leaving the Congregation, I will cover in the next part of my book.

MY LIFE OUT THE CONGREGATION (IN BRAZIL)

As you read before, my first step in leaving the Congregation was when I asked for a one year leave of absence. I went to Uruacu, Goias with the other sister to start a new Congregation, but I gave up on that idea. I decided not to go with Mother Felcicidade to Rio Grande do Sul, but instead tried to find a secular institute, rather than returning to the same Congregation that I had left.

With the help of a priest friend of mine, I made contact with SEARA, a new Secular institute, and went to Ponta Grossa, Parana. Believe it or not I traveled 30 hours with 4 bus connections, because I was still in Uruacu Goias.

In Ponta Grossa I met the priest and four ladies. In December or January I would go to live in Chapeco, Santa Catarina. But for the meantime I returned to Uruacu. I felt I was about to begin another big adventure, because some time later I heard that the new Secular Institute was not doing well.

At the end of my one year absence from the Congregation I needed to go back to Rio de Janeiro, although in my mind I was prepared to move to Chapeco, SC. But when I arrived in Rio de Janeiro, I decided to give myself one more time at the same Congregation. I felt all the sisters and the new Mother General were so happy to see me back, and my Spiritual director encouraged me to stay.

Really when I saw the sisters so happy to see me back, I asked myself were they really happy for me? Or really was it a sign of hypocrisy, because I was at the side of Mother Felicidade when I left. And now I was back, and she had started the new Congregation. Ok, I can say I accepted the manifestation of happiness with me, and I stayed. I gave myself one year to try again.

I was transferred to Heliopolis, Rio de Janeiro, to Las Escola Sao Judas Tadeu. The Mother General asked me to be the Principal of the School, because the former Principal was leaving the Congregation, too. And the Community elected me to be the Superior of the Community.

Can you believe that? I had been one year absent from the Congregation. I decided to come back and they asked me to be the Principal of the School and the Community elected me to be the Superior?. I can say it was too much for my mind. And another thing happened. In April they received a donation of $91,000.00 dollars from Switzerland, to finish the construction of the Orphanage.

Of course I could manage that money, and really the building turned out beautifully. We had at that time around 50 girls at that internate, and the school was doing well in the poor neighborhoods around it.

I can tell that at that time I was starting to feel empty inside myself. I was feeling even worse the big division within the Congregation. In this year, 1981, I started getting in contact with another secular Institute, in Belo Horizonte, MG, named UNITAS. It was originally from the Netherlands. I felt at that time I made a good choice. I met Mary, a member of the Institute, and before I had left the Congregation I had attended some meetings in Belo Horizonte and was very happy.

I used lot of diplomacy when leaving of the Congregation. At that time the Diocese of Rio de Janeiro was extremely concerned about the increasing number of the sisters leaving. I went twice to the Çardinal residence and talked with an Auxiliary Bishop. When I officially sent my letters they approved me very quickly and easily.

Then on December 19th, 1981, I left the Convent and went to my Mother's house. I continued to be the Principal at Lar Escola Sao Judas Tadeu for one more year, until 1982. When I say I lived in the Convent for 20 years and 8 months I count from April 20th, 1961 until December 19th, 1981 (of course one day before completing the eight months).

I chose that day, December 19th, because I wanted to go to a family party, at my cousin Luiz Cesar's house. It was so great for me meet my family again. They were celebrating his mother, Aunt Cecy's 70th birthday and all the family birthdays in December.

In 1982 I continued to work at the Lar Escola Sao Judas Tadeu. At the end of the year I decided submit my resignation, at the same time I asked to definitely leave the Congregation, because I was only exclausted. I said before I was going to go to Belo Horizonte, to a meeting at UNITAS, but I decided to give up that, too, and said to myself: Forget trying to find a simple Institution to belong to -- BE YOURSELF, MARTA. Because if you are part of any Institution is like you have a label on yourself.

When I left my job as the Principal at Lar Escola Sao Judas Tadeu, with the money I received, I paid off my contribution to the social security in my Country (INPS) since Jan 1964, when I took my first Vows.

Then after one week vacation, with my friend Neida, in Cabo Frio, my cousin Laura Monte Mor was looking for me. She knew I had the Registry to be Principal of a School, and the CENEC (Company National of Community School), urgently needed a Principal for a School in Santa Cruz da Serra, Rio de Janeiro. Then I started my work at the Cenecista School in Santa Cruz da Serra.

It was another novel in my life. The School was without a Principal and with a lot of problems with the Secretary of Education. I needed a job, so I decided to accept.

The School was far from my Mother's house, where I was living at that time, but I assumed the responsibility. They told me I didn't need to go every single day, but I felt I really needed to go Monday through Friday, because the situation there was not very good.

They had Elementary and Ginasio (1st to 8th grade) and two classes of the last year of High School (a Teacher course and an Accounting course) but those 2 high school courses were not approved by the Secretary of Education. The school had already graduated one of its classes and now it was impossible for those students to have their certificates registered.

My Lord! What a work! There was a man named J.M. who did the Administrative work at the School, I was only the Principal. Thank God, the State Supervisor at that time, Sonia, knew me from before and trusted me. And of course the work I had to regularize the situation of that school was incredibly hard. It was not until the end of 1984 that I finally won.

J.M., the Administrator of the School, gave me a very, very hard time. All the banks required our two signatures; this was normal at many institutions. J.M. dealt with the finances, I only signed with him. He was responsible to know if we had money in the bank or not, to pay the employees, for example.

But twice it happened that he left 2 checks for me to sign, I gave the employees the checks without money in the bank.

The third time this happened, I got nervous and wrote to the administration of the CENEC about the situation. J.M. received a letter back from the CENEC, who wanted an explanation and he resigned. Then the administration of the CENEC asked me to handle the two positions, Principal and administrator. I said alone, I couldn't; it would be possible only if I had an assistant. I gave Neida's name. They accepted and we started to work together.

Then, Neida and I became roommates. We rented a small apartment in Santa Cruz da Serra. Every weekend I went to my mother's house at Tijuca, so that she could accept the idea that I was living away again.

The first reason for renting an apartment in Santa Cruz da Serra was to be closer to the school, which really needed more attention. The second reason was that I had lived more than 20 years away from my family, and it was difficult again to be home. I had started to be independent and my father was not there any more...

I worked at the Cenecista School in Santa Cruz da Serra until the end of 1984, when unfortunately the school was closed. I say unfortunately because that school was attended by approximately 500 children, most of them poor. But for political reasons, inside de Estadual Administration of the CENEC, they decided close the school. Instead of borrowing for the School 14,000 cruzeiros to cover the school's debt, they decided spend 50,000 cruzeiros to cover severance pay for the employees.

We decided to move from Santa Cruz da Serra, which was a small town. We rented an apartment at Duque de Caxias City. I would not have felt comfortable if we had remained near the school. It was like a small village, where everybody knows everybody and I was always close and friendly with the children and their families.

The new apartment was bigger than the first one, with 2 bedrooms. Neida's sister Lucilia came to live with us, with her 3 kids. They stayed only for 6 months. Vivia was 5 years old. The 2 older ones, in between studying and work, it was not easy to do. They went back to Divinopolis.

Neida started working at Plank Eisten School, in Copacabana. She was the Secretary of the School. I stayed for 6 months looking for a job. It was for me a time that I felt myself without power. It is hard to write about, because we had Lucilia and children with us.

Then finally in July 1985 I started working at the Day Care (Creche) at the Instituto Isabel. I was like a director, or coordinator. Can you imagine that? In 1983 when we rented the apartment in Santa Cruz da Serra, it was because we would be closer to our work place. Now we were living in Duque de Caxias and Neida gets work in Copacabana, and I get mine at Tijuca. Then suddenly I had the idea to live in my own apartment in S. Ivo Building, at Tijuca.

My apartment was rented to Vilma Viola, had lived there for 28 years, and she almost had a Heart Attack when I went to talk with her, to tell her that I needed to live in my apartment. She asked me to give her some more time to move.

Then in November we moved to my Mother's apartment and only in February 1985 we moved to my apart, #403. But the things happening in my life were so amazing that nobody would believe. A good friend of mine, Helena Costa, an ex-nun, came to my house and gave me an offer to work where she was working at CIDADE DOS MENINOS (Boy's City), in Caxias. I would be a Director of one division, named INSTITUTO PROVEDORA MARGARIDA ARAUJO.

In that division we had girls from 3 years to 12 years old, and boys 3 to 7 years old. Boy's City had 4 divisions, only that one with girls, the other ones with boys, and most of them orphans or from very bad family situations. It was like a big farm, where the boys were trained to produce vegetables, and many othe professions. I worked there only a few months, from March to November 1986, because, again I was far away from my work, and I saw many other situations I could not accept.

I took the place of Sr. Cecilia, who had been there for 10 years. It was not very easy to work there. The discipline lady had resigned when Sr. Cecilia left. Then Neida was admitted and we worked together again.

But after so many impositions from the Director General of this place, I submitted my resignation. I really enjoyed working with those children, some of whom were abandoned. I felt the policy of that place was not intended to protect the poor children, but their own pocketbooks.

I decided to open, with Neida, a Mini Day Care, at my apartment in Tijuca. That was our last work in Brazil. And it was a marvelous experience. We would have made better money if it had been a big place, like a house. It lasted only about four months.

You can see that after I left the Congregation I worked here and there, and I did not establish myself economically. I decided to go to America, looking first for a better economical life.

MY LIFE IN AMERICA (CHICAGO)

Everybody is curious to know why I decided come to live in America, and always I have the answer "I came to find a better economical situation."

And really that's what was happening. When I left the convent I was 40th. At that age, in my country, it was almost impossible to find a reasonable job. After 6 years of trying, I decided to make a big change in my life and come to America.

I had no experience with passports or visas. At that time there was a lot of talk about Brazilian people coming to America. I was amazed and decided to do that.

At this time I was running the Mini Day Care in my apartment at Tijuca. While talking with Maria da Graca, my youngest sister, she asked me why I did not sell my apartment and buy a house. Her father in law was selling his house at Praca da Bandeira. Suddenly I had the idea to sell my apartment, buy a smaller one, and with the difference in money I would go to America.

I thought, but not only thought, because they say in my Language "…of thinking…the donkey died…" and I started to act. This conversation with Maria da Graca happened at the end of March. The Mini Day Care was open until the end of April. In May I decided to sell the apartment, put everything away from the Day Care, and our personal belongs, like furniture.

But it was not an easy time to sell property in my country. It was a time of economic change. Nobody was selling or buying. It was interesting, my next door neighbor, at apt 401, Sr. Arlindo, a Portuguese man, asked me about how much I was asking for the apartment. He said had a friend interested.

On July 2nd I met him again in the street, and he asked me the same question about my apartment. I answer him back "Sr. Arlindo, is it you who is interested in buying my apartment?" He smiled and said "Yes."

Then finally I negotiated with him. He had a small apartment at Vicente Carvalho. We made an exchange. He bought mine and I bought the small one. He paid the difference in price, around $ 6,000.00 dollars, because mine was big and in Tijuca, a better location.

It was the easy way I found. I sold my apartment but still had an apartment in Brazil. With the money I received I could come and still lend for Neida. To come to America by myself would be awfully hard.

After that everything went smoothly. With passports in hand we went to a travel agency. They sent somebody to the American Consulate to get the visa, which was a Multiple Visa for 4 years. I proved I had money in the bank, and so on, and Neida come as a companion for me. Everything was all set for us to come to America. Now we had to decide WHERE to go.

I had a meeting with Beth Lins, a good friend of my nieces Denise and Janete. She had lived in the USA for 2 years. At the time we met Beth we were thinking to go to the Boston area, where Maria dos Anjos were.

M.D. came in January 1987. I spoke with her by phone about my intention to go. I had money enough for a couple months, but? Nothing happened, because she couldn't help me. She was planning to come back to Brazil.

But I always, always was a persistent person. Beth gave me some names and addresses of friends of hers still in Chicago. I wrote to Celia Nascimento asking her about the possibility of a baby sitting job.

And it was funny, it was in July 1987 when I called M.D., and it was the day before my trip to Guaxupe when she gave me a negative answer. Then on the same day I wrote to Celia Nascimento, and in Guaxupe I told everyone I was coming to BOSTON.

This trip was during a weekend. I went with my sisters Diva and Zulmira to visit my brother Ismail who was living in Guaxupe with Maria Angela, his second wife. I had the opportunity to say goodbye to my family there.

The day after I came back from Guaxupe, I received a phone call from Celia. She called me at Maria da Graca's house. I talked with Visnja (with my broken English, but I got by) and finally everything was all set. I would go at the end of September, and be a baby sitter for Lella and Nika, because Celia was coming back to Brazil after 4 years in America.

Some days later I received a letter from Celia, with a lot of information about the job at the Gembick's, and the address of L.M., who would receive us in Chicago.

Soon I had to empty apartment 403. We moved to my mother's house until the day we traveled. We got the visa on September 1st, and booked the ticket for September 23rd, a Wednesday.

We went for one week to Cabo Frio, and stayed with Margareth, Neida's niece. I remember on September 6th I came back to Rio de Janeiro to go on a pilgrimage to Aparecida do Norte with my two sisters, Diva and Zulmira. At the bus station I met Celia and her mother. She said to me" Marta, I don't have good news for you. Visnja called me and decided hire another Brazilian girl named Elza."

And do you believe it or not I did not get disturbed, because I had the visa, had already bought the tickets, and had already written to Luis Mussi. I said to myself "God will take care of me." Then I went on the pilgrimage to Our Lady of Aparecida. I prayed and enjoyed staying with my 2 sisters. We went by bus from the St. Francis Xavier Parish.

After that we went to Divinopolis to say goodbye to Neida's family. It was quick because we had no more time. By then we needed to get rid of everything we had at my apartment. We sold some things, but we gave a lot of things to Luiza, Neida's sister, because she was moving to Cabo Frio. It was great for me. It was like to give up everything I had a second time; first was when I went to the Convent and now moving to America. I hoped a New Horizon would open for me.

Now I need to talk a little more about Beth Lins. She was a friend of my niece Denise. They worked together at a small kindergarten school at Urca. She was also a good friend of Janete. I don't remember having met her before, but I remember my sister Zulmira (mother of Denise and Janete) talking a lot about her, how she was a great support for Denise when she divorced the first time. Beth was always a kind and affectionate person.

When she came to America, she was going to take a course at a Montessori School, to become a teacher. At that time she was working at an American School in Rio de Janeiro. She stayed in the USA for about 2 ½ years. Then she met Cor, a man from the Netherlands. They got married in Brazil in July 1987, at almost the time she helped me to come to America. Before she moved to the Netherlands, I think in September 1987, she knew that Visnja, the mother of Nika and Lella, had chosen the other younger Brazilian girl instead of me. She sent a gift for the 2 girls, because she really wanted Visnja to meet me. It was interesting to me, that idea.

With the visa and tickets in hand we started to pack. We packed a lot of winter clothes because I was afraid of Chicago's cold weather.

I went to say goodbye to my aunts and uncles at Copacabana. They tried to give me a great support. I went to Aunt Dedete's house, too, in Ipanema. She was very happy with my decision. She said I was a brave woman, like my father always was. It made me so happy.

Denise made a farewell dinner with the "Urca residents", as I used to call Zulmira's family. One week before my departure we had a farewell lunch at my mother's house.

Finally the day of our trip arrived. We traveled by TransBrasil, direct to Orlando, Florida. We had reservations there at a hotel for 3 weeks.

The flight was at 9:00 AM. My sister Maria da Graca, her husband and her son Marcelo (my youngest nephew), gave us a ride to the airport. I remember, Marcelo, somehow sad (he was not 5 years old yet) asked" Aunt Neida , when you come back I will be still a young boy?" He loves Neida and me.

Some months before we made for him a clown costume. With colored papers, we drew his face, put a big nose. We took a picture and he said "Aunt Neida, the costume doesn't work good for me, because I am still scared of clowns." Look at the sincerity of a child: we dressed him like a clown, but he did not feel like a clown.

Life? Say Yes to Life

We did not have any problem during our departure, because our luggage was at the correct weight. The airplane left at 9:00 AM sharp. Everything was new for us, especially for my friend Neida. She never flew before and for me this was my first international experience.

The airplane was almost full. We made friends with a man named Feijo (who wasn't the Antonio Feijo). He was very helpful to us because he knew Orlando. I showed him the name and address of the hotel and the car rental agency where we had reservations. He made me a map with the location where we would pick up the car and directions to the hotel in Kissimmee.

When we arrived, we had to go through Customs, take the luggage and so on. We had never had that experience before, and at that time, believe or not, I had to go to the bathroom (pee.), and I had to keep myself in a good shape. They took my passport and Neida's and stamped the visa for 6 months and said to us "Good luck!" I took a deep breath; I was free (ahahah) to go to the bathroom. After that, we took the luggage and went to the car rental agency and then to the hotel.

Since that first time, Oh My Lord, difficult it was to understand the English language. It seemed to me I had never heard a word of it before then.

I never had driven an automatic car. Can you believe I did not know how to start the car? I decided to go back inside the Alamo Agency and ask for help. I met a young man and started to try explain to him my problem and he was paying too much attention to my words (broken, of course). Then, I put my hands at my waist, and I asked in my own language" Listen, do you speak Portuguese? And are you from Minas Gerais?" He smiled and said "Yes" and we laughed a lot and he came to help me. We had arrived on the same flight.

We left the Alamo, took the map they gave to me and the map from Mr. Feijo. I took the Expressway, paid the toll and kept going. After half an hour driving, it started to rain a little, and we didn't know how to turn on the wipers. I said to Neida"its better we don't get nervous. At the first opportunity we need to stop and ask for help."

Then we saw a hotel on the right side of the road. I drove close to the building, and a security guard comes to us. Then my first dumb question:" Do you speak English?" Of course I want ask "Do you speak only English?" He laughed and help us with the car,. Then I asked about the hotel we were supposed to go to. He said "It is over there," and pointed at the hotel on the other side of the road. We were in front of the Hotel! I was so happy that I couldn't express my feelings and could only say"Oh! No!" and he said "Oh, Yes. It is over there!" It was funny because he thought I did not believe him. Finally I thanked him and drove to the hotel.

At the hotel I can't say how many confusions we had: to find the room, to find a vending machine (we were hungry, it was later then midnight). The next morning we faced a new communication barrier. We were hungry and needed to find a place for breakfast. We spent most of the day at the hotel because we were afraid to get lost. At night I had to call my mother at my sister's house. This was another big trouble for us. I couldn't call from the room because I didn't understand a word the operator said. I went to the switchboard and someone helped me and I spoke with my mother and told her everything was going right for me and Neida.

The next day we went to the Disney World. Everything was new for us. We stayed amazed and happy, and decided we had to come back there. The next day we went to the Epcot Center. It was amazing, too.

Saturday we had to buy the plane tickets to Chicago and call L.M. to confirm we would arrive on Sunday. Sunday we brought the car back to Alamo and flew to Chicago. It was a quick trip, peaceful. When we arrived in Chicago, we took a cab to L.M.'s house.

As soon as we arrived, he invited us to go shopping at the supermarket to buy the groceries. It was fine for us, because since we arrived we started to divide everything. The next day we went with him to Clarendon Hills, to the Gembick's house.

That first interview with the family was great. Visnja and Stanley talked with me and L.M. helped to translate. I met the girls, and I gave them the gifts from Beth Lins. The next day Luiz brought me to Clarendon Hills and Neida stayed with him in Chicago.

L.M. was a great support for us in Chicago. Neida stay with him. He found a job for her at the same cleaning company where he worked. After one month, Neida had a full time job. It was not an easy job, but she was happy.

Now I need talk about the Gembick family, and about what happened when I was planning come work as a babysitter, but they decided to get the other younger Brazilian girl. I completely understood Visnija's situation.

With the babysitter before Celia, she had a big problem. The Brazilian lady, from Bahia, was 50th years old, didn't speak English and did not drive a car. And thought, I was away, with my 46^{t} years, with broken English. I said I could drive a car, but the other had said the same. At that time Visnja met a younger Brazilian, with better English, and she was already in USA, so she decided to hire the younger one, named Elza.

But she stayed only one week. Visnja knew I was arriving at L.M.'s house in Chicago, and she called me for interview.

This happened because Elza wanted to study English full time at College of De Page. The schedule of the 2 girls, Nika and Lella, was hard to coordinate with a full time course load. She must have had other personal problems, because she was crying all day long, maybe homesick for her family and boyfriend in Brazil.

Then I arrived and Visnja decided to hire me, but she was remained there for 10 days, so I could get familiar with the girls' routine, and with the housework which would be done once a week.

I adjusted to my new job very easily with no big trouble about the language. I started to hear and re-peat, and soon I went to school to take classes of English as a Second Language at Hinsdale High School. I started at Level 3 and continued until level 8 at College of Du Page.

The first phase of my life in America, when I worked with the Gembick family, was a great experience for me. Visnja was always very kind and friendly and Stanley was a sweet person. It was funny, I never called him by his first name, but always Mister Stanley. It was completely wrong in the English language, but? It was me.

It was at Chicago, 1989, with the Gembicki family at the Farewell dinner

Even now I am always in contact and maintain a great friendship with the Gembicks. I used to say "They are my first American family."

Nika was always whining, and loved to dominate the babysitters. Lella, when I first came, was somewhat distant from the babysitters, but soon I conquered her and she became very friendly with me. At that time Nika was 6th and Lella was 8th. Later I would talk more about my life with the 2 little ones.

I usually stayed in Clarendon Hills until Friday night when I was going to Chicago, and came back Sunday night, and usually traveled by train.

Neida lived with L.M. until December 87. It was a nice time but we did not have in mind to go back to Brazil. We decided to rent an apartment in Chicago. Neida would be there during the week and every weekend I would be there. Then on December 20th we made our first move in the USA. The apartment was on the same street as Luiz's apartment. It was 1941 West Ohio St

Near Christmas time the Gembick family went to Florida for 2 weeks. I stayed there at Clarendon Hills. It was not easy and somewhat scary, because it was my first winter and snow.

On Christmas Eve, Dec 24th, Neida had to work until 11 PM. She could get the last train to Clarendon Hills at 11:30PM. I was not sure if she would come or not to Clarendon Hills. I went to my bedroom, left all the lights on but I fell asleep watching the Mass at the Vatican. When Neida arrived, it was snowing. She rang the bell, but no answer. Then she knocked on a window close to my bedroom and finally I woke up. She was almost frozen and hungry, but we stayed together for our 1st Christmas in the USA.

On Christmas Day I invited L.M. to come and had dinner with me and Neida, in Clarendon Hills. We had a turkey the family left for me.

The Gembick family would return from Florida on January 1st. I think Visnja was sorry I would be staying home alone. She called me and told me to go to Chicago on the afternoon of the 31st so I could stay with Neida on New Year's Eve.

And we kept going living our lives. In 1988 I was in Clarendon Hills and Neida in Chicago, working at the cleaning company. In May we moved to 921 N Damen Ave, because the apartment was smaller and cheaper. Gentil helped Neida to move.

One Saturday in April, Sofia, Gentil's wife, had to go work, and had no baby sitter for the 2 little girls, Gisele and Elisangela. I stayed home with them, and from then we began a great friendship.

At that time in Chicago I met some Brazilian friends who were working at the same company as Neida, Amaro and his wife, Eneida, Rose, Marilyn and Ari. Neida met Pedro, who became her boyfriend. He liked me and sometimes he gave me a ride back to Clarendon Hills on Sunday Night. We went places together, like the Sears tower, Brookfield Zoo, and to a Mexican Party Fiesta del Sol. Christmas 1988 we spent together with L.M. at our apartment in Chicago.

I was never happy when Neida was working at that cleaning company, because the work was hard, and she did not have time and disposition to go to English Class. Finally in 1989, on January 2nd, she started working as a babysitter for the Nordin family in Lisle.

I mentioned before about Elza, the Brazilian who was with the Gembicks one week before I arrived in USA. I stayed in touch with her, by phone, and at the College of Du Page. She decided go back to Brazil for good, and Neida took her place as babysitter for the 2 children, 8 month old Christina, and 4 year old Steve. The father was a lawyer and the mother a doctor, and they needed a baby sitter during the week, and sometimes on Saturdays.

We start 1989 with a new enthusiasm. Neida worked in Lisle, which was not far from Clarendon Hills, around 15 minutes by car. We worked Monday to Friday, coming back and forth to Chicago together. Neida was using the car of the family, and when she worked on Saturdays, I went there, slept and stayed there with them.

I think it was at that time or in November 1988 we started our process of Legalization. I will tell about that later, when I need to express my gratitude to Eneida, Amaro's wife, who suggested to us the possibility that we could get our papers.

I decided to go to Brazil to visit my mother for the first time, and I decided to leave the Gembick family. Neida, for other reasons, left the Nordin on the same day, June 16, 1989. I had a ticket to go to my country the next day.

My first visit to Brazil was when I had completed 1 year and 9 months in the USA. I was leaving the Gembick family, because with the Employment Authorization in hand, I was dreaming of a better job.

My trip was only for 3 weeks. My mother was doing well still, only starting to lose her eyesight. Andre, my nephew, was living with her.

Then we had an idea, to get somebody as a companion for her. We tried to bring Neida's niece, Beatriz, but she did not stay for long.

I had an opportunity to visit my aunts and uncles in Copacabana. They were so happy with me. At that time Aunt Irenita was alive.

At my Mother's house they made a big dinner for me "Cozido" and I videotaped that opportunity to have my family together.

I had a very calm 3 weeks there. I went to visit the nuns at the Institute Isabel, and went to visit some other friends, too.

At that time I had 3 grand niece and nephews, Tianna and Mariana, Zulmira's grand kids, and Bruno, Ivinho's grand kid, they were one year old. I went to Mariana's Birthday Party. They were living at that time in Santa Teresa. Before I came to America I already had 2 grand nephews, Pedro, who was Ismail's grand son, living in Recife, PE and Joao Carlos, who was Paulo's grand son, living in Pocos de Caldas, MG.

When I came back from Brazil, I started a new stage of my life in Chicago. But before that I need to talk about Joe, in my life.

When I was in Clarendon Hills, preparing to go to Brazil, Mauro, my nephew, wrote me a letter, asking me to buy for him some accessories for his camera. I went to a store where I had bought my camera. It was a very nice store.

I was there to buy not only one camera, but several things, and they would be expensive. The owner of the store came to talk with me, and I had to return there 2 or 3 times, and that person was very interested to talk with me. Of course I said I was going to Brazil, to visit my mother and family, and that after I would stay in Chicago, looking for another job. He asked me for my phone number and address, the details of my travel, my departure and return dates.

When I commented with Neida about that man, she said "Wow, Marta! He is interested in you" and I said "No way! He is only asking me questions because I am buying a lot things and he needs to know my address after my trip." But the first phone call I received when I just arrived home was from him. He wanted to know how was my trip, and so on.

In our lives we have good moments and some not that good, and in some cases we do like "break the head," because we think we own the TRUTH, and sometimes all the world. At that time my English was not very good.

When I returned from my trip Neida and I started to look for new jobs. Of course I cannot say everything in here, because it would be a new novel. I got it into my mind that if I bought a car, it would be easier. Joe tried to help me to find a reasonable car with the amount of money we had in hand.

Then one day he called me saying he had 4 tickets for a baseball game at Cubs Stadium. Before the game he came to my apartment and had dinner with me and Neida. We went to the Cubs' Stadium, only him, Neida and me, because Luiz couldn't come with us. It was funny I didn't understand anything about a baseball game, but it was interesting and I enjoyed it.

After that we talked several times by phone, and I had some lenses that Mauro sent back. Nick decided to come to Chicago, and we went for a dinner at a Chinese Restaurant. It was a tremendous coincidence, because Neida was starting work, that night on the night shift, taking care of an old lady, 3 blocks away from our place.

After dinner he decided to come to the apartment. He was interested to see some videostapes I brought from Brazil. He was enthusiastic to learn Portuguese; he knew seven languages already.

It was a new stage in my life, because I had never had the feeling that a man was interested in me, because remember, when I went to the convent, I had never had a boyfriend. After I left the convent, I never gave myself that possibility. I would say, I am not sure, ashamed? Of my face? I really don't know for sure.

Of course I saw him a couple other times, until we moved to Florida. Still after that we kept in touch by phone and we developed a nice friendship. Joe had been a wonderful person in my life.

It was not easy finding a job after I came back from Brazil. I knew the Gembick family would give a good recommendation for me.

In September I went to Barrington, to work for 10 days taking care of 2 kids, Jenny , a sweet girl almost 3 years old, and JP, a boy almost 5, because the parents were going to travel to Hawaii.

It was a different experience, but I promised myself I never would do that again. The kids didn't know me, I was a stranger to them (and with broken English….) and I was alone. The house was a very big mansion and the car? Oh Brother! I never drove a car like that before. But I won, made things right, and the parents were very happy when they come back, and I was feeling free.

At that time Neida was working in Bensenville, at Michael's house she was living in, Monday to Saturday. After Barrington I tried to take care of Michael's mother, but it lasted only one week.

After that I had an opportunity to work at a factory. It was a Bijouterie Factory. I worked there almost 2 months. It was interesting for me, the experience of working in a factory. My shift was 8 am to 4 PM. We had to put the bijouterie in pad or box, and label them with the prices to make them ready to go to the stores. I felt great there.

After that I went work in Buffalo Grove, taking care of a baby, Michael Ross. He was a beautiful 3 months old boy. I stayed there Sunday night to Friday night, when I went to Chicago. Neida came back on Saturdays from Benseville.

And at that time we met N.S., who invited and convinced us to move to Florida, and it was a great adventure. Of course I will tell you about that in the next part.

FLORIDA

How was the time we lived in Florida for us? I think that everyone knows, so far, that if sometimes I use the word "we" or "us," especially after I came to America, I refer to Neida and me. We have a great and wonderful friendship. Most of the time in Florida and after that we've worked at the same places.

We started thinking of moving to Florida. It was like running away, or leaving behind the winter of Chicago; too much cold and wind. Florida was like, for us, entering into a paradise. But what kind of a paradise was waiting for us? I could say we entered a Lost Paradise.

Really it was not only running away from the cold weather. It was that they convinced us with what they said about Florida, that we could find better jobs, better money. But we were not making bad money in Chicago. They said to us still transit (?), the traffic was better in Florida, and so on. So we went.

The only thing good was the weather. It was almost like Rio de Janeiro, where I was born and raised. There were many beautiful views. But what a big deception we had about almost all the other points they said was great. We lived in Florida one year and one month in Tampa and one week in Gainesville. We had nothing but trouble from the first to the last day in Florida.

Well I don't want stop only at the negative points, because I think we need to put, or better say, we need to look at things in a positive way. I remember when I was teaching Religion, or Civics, in my country. I used to say to my students: When we need to write a mathematical sign (+), what do you write first? It is a minus sign (-) and then you cross that and have (+). What's happening? You start with a (-) and then you cross that and have a (+). Sometimes from a bad situation (-) , you can get a better one with a (+).

OK, we left Chicago on February 14, 1990, in the middle of a big snowstorm. Our friends Gentil and Sofia gave us a ride to Union Station, and believe it or not it took us 1 1/12 hours. The train was 3 hours delayed. It was very confusing, especially for my head. We left Chicago with a connection in Washington DC, and then to Waldo, Florida.

Around 5 am, because of the delay to leave Chicago, they called us to have breakfast and get off the train in Pittsburgh, to take a bus to get to Washington DC on time for the next connection to Florida. There were about 20 of us.

At a certain point it was wonderful, because we got to Washington DC by bus and we had a better panoramic view than if we had gone by train. Union Station there was beautiful; it had been reconstructed at that time.

We arrived in Waldo, Florida at 6.00 am on February, 16. N.S. was waiting for us, because Waldo was the closest train Station to Gainesville, where he was living. Oh! Gosh, it is hard to remember about that first day in Florida, but anyway I need to talk about Napoleao, who obviously was not the BONAPARTE, right?

I remember one evening in September or October of 1989, when I was getting home. Mrs. Amalia, who was our landlord and very good friend, she said she met a Brazilian man, born in Brazil and raised in the USA. She said he was a very nice person, very intelligent, but he was so lonely because his mother passed away not so long ago. She asked me if she could give our telephone number to him, and I said that would be no problem, because we speak the same language, and we would help him. Then some weeks later, he came to our house (without calling before) on a Saturday, and he stayed talking and talking with me and Neida until past 12:00 am.

Sincerely, he gave the impression that he was very intelligent, and had a sense of life. He seemed to have great knowledge about everything we talked about. He came to the USA when he was 12 years old, and was educated here. He was so enthusiastic when he found out we were nuns before. Only later we discovered he was a religious fanatic.

The next day, Sunday, he picked us up at 11:00 am to go to Mass, and then to a lot of other churches. Then he took his friend Ted, who was from Poland, and brought us to a Polish Restaurant in Niles. Then we went to the cemetery where his mother was, and he took us to the cinema, because at the night before I said we had not been to a cinema since we came to the USA. After that he came back again to our apartment and stayed talking and talking until very late again. He said he was deciding whether to move to Florida with Ted and another Polish friend. He spoke the Polish language fluently, because his parents were immigrants from Poland to Brazil.

Two or 3 weeks after that Napoleao moved to Florida. He always called us on the phone, giving us great news, so enthusiastic he was about being there. So we decided to go to live in Florida, because if it had better weather, it would have better jobs. We decided to get rid of everything we had. We sold and gave away many things too. We sold the car, at the time it was the second car we had, which I named "segundinho" (the second one), and we still bought with us 9 packages to the train.

The day we arrived in Florida we went directly to his apartment where he was living. It was a condominium, with a great appearance. The apartment had 2 bedrooms and 2 bathrooms. But he only had one chair and one bean bag chair. It was yellow and he named it "banana". In his bedroom he had an airbed, and we brought from Chicago 2 airbeds for ourselves. In the kitchen there was nothing to eat, because he always ate canned food, heated in the microwave. No coffee, nothing, could you imagine? We came from a 30 hour trip, exhausted and hungry, and nothing to eat!!!!!!

We took showers and he brought us to have lunch at a restaurant, he paid. Then we went to Jacksonville, where he was working, to receive his paycheck. Then he took us to St Augustine, Palatka, and then we came home. By then it was after 8:00 PM. From that first day we started not believing him, but we wanted to try to believe. He said he was unemployed.

He worked with asbestos (to remove the asbestos) and then he started to say there would be more opportunities for better jobs for us and for him in a big city like Tampa, Orlando or Jacksonville. We said OK, because we needed the best for all 3. If in other places we would have better conditions, why not go?

The next Sunday he took us to church, of course he needed to keep up his image of a good Catholic man for us. After the Mass we went to a shopping center to buy chairs, some kitchen things, like pans, plates, cups, silverware and a coffee maker and did some grocery shopping, too. The next day we decided go to Palatka and see about the possibility of moving there. Before we left Gainesville, N.S. stopped at a MacDonald's for lunch (Neida and I had eat home but he did not).

He bought a lunch for him and a soda for us, and we sat at an outside table. It was a very great place, the weather perfect. Then he started his rosary of Lamentation. He said was late 2 months of rent, 2 or 3 months' telephones bills, and so on. He was in need of $900 dollars, and he said he would pay us back in 2 months. Believe it or not he started to cry, the tears were running down his face. He was saying that entire situation started after his mother died, when he needed to borrow money for the funeral. Then what happened? We felt sorry for him, and gave him the money. He became like a new man again.

When we were leaving for Palatka he stoped at the house of two American friends of his, David and Hart. They worked together in Jacksonville. He said those two friends wanted live with us, because we could divide the rent 5 ways instead of 3. That's fine, we said. Always we were saying yes to all his suggestions.

I should mention that the Polish men from Chicago, they gave up and one went back to Chicago and I think the other one to Poland (N.S. told us that). We went to Palatka, saw 2 or 3 apartments, and thank God we convinced him it was a small town too, and maybe without possibility for better jobs.

On Wednesday N.S. and David went to Tampa by themselves to look for jobs and a place to rent. They came back very happy because they said they found a job for all 3 of them starting next week. They brought a lot of flyers and newspapers with advertisements about condominiums and houses for renting. The next day we made our packages again.

On Friday, Feb 23rd, the day we were completed two years and five months in America, we left for Tampa, with N.S. and David. We made sure we had all our baggage with us. We left only one box with kitchen stuffs, the TV, and another box with winter clothes.

We left Gainesville at 7:30 AM and after 3 hours we arrived in Tampa, like it was a GREAT MISSION, looking for an apartment to rent, we drove around and around. First they said Clearwater was a good place, and then we went to Oldsmar. It was almost 6:00 pm and we still had not found anything with a reasonable price. I forgot to say it was raining all day long. They thought it was that easy: stop at a condominium, look, talk, pay and get into an apartment. But it wasn't. We had arrived in a new city without references, Neida and I at that time without credit or bank accounts in that city, and we didn't know anything about their references. Neida and I decided to stay in a hotel in Tampa, and they would return the next morning to start the search again. Finally they left us at a Hotel on Route 275.

Sincerely I almost started to panic! I felt so small and stupid. I had always that I was an intelligent person, making many difficult decisions in my life, and now I felt myself in the hands of those men? We reached the conclusion that they didn't have any money of their own and were counting only on our money. I cried so much; thank God I didn't have a heart attack. We decided not to stay with Napoleao and his friends; we would rent a place of our own.

The next day, Saturday, they arrived at 9:00 am. We called only N.S. to our room and gave him our decision, that Neida and I would live together without him and his friends. At one point I said that they were looking for expensive places to live which we could not afford. He appeared so understanding and said David knew the Tampa area very well and would help us to find a place for the two of us. He immediately took the newspaper and made a phone call, and made an appointment to see a place.

We paid the hotel, took our luggage again and left. The apartment was at East Louisiana Ave. It was in an old house, divided into 3 apartments. The appearance of the house was not that good but the apartment included furniture, which we needed. The owner was an old man, a very nice person whose English was difficult for us to understand, or maybe our language was not that good at that time. But we rented it. The apartment he showed us was on the second floor, with 2 bedrooms. It was kind of large for us, but it was $290 per month and $150 deposit. When we finished signing the papers, he gave us the keys and receipt.

Then David and N.S. asked him to show the other apartment on the first floor. It had only one bed room, but was better looking, and it was $190 per month and $100 deposit. Neida almost lost her mind, because they said to the owner they wanted to rent that apartment. We hadn't even known the owner had 2 apartments to rent. Our luggage was already in the apartment on the 2nd floor. We had the key and receipt and the old man really did not understand anything.

They went back to Gainesville, and Napoleao asked me for 50 dollars more. He said they would be backing Monday because they would start work on Wednesday, and they would bring the kitchen stuff and TV for us.

On Monday we called the owner and explained to him our reason to move into the smaller apartment, and he accepted. We called the electric, gas and telephone Company. Now we needed to find jobs.

The most of the advertised jobs we found were for housekeeping in the hotels, because Tampa was a tourist place. We started applying for jobs, but it was very difficult, because public transportation in Tampa was limited to certain times.

N.S. come back only the next weekend, brought our kitchen stuffs and the next Monday he gave us a ride to make applications at 5 hotels.

The next Wednesday we received an answer from Holiday Inn that we would start Friday for 3 training days. We decided to buy a car, because it would be too hard to get there by bus. So we went walking on Florida Avenue, not far from where we lived, looking for car dealers. We bought our 1st car in Florida, a Toyota Corolla 76. It was so junky and so many problems running that we named it SAFIRENTO (we used to call kids "Safirento" when they were spoiled).

We started working at Holiday Inn on March 9. Now I don't want talk about the housekeeping work at the Hotel, it was very hard for me, but I won. We worked there one year and some days, and then we asked to move to Massachusetts.

Before I finish talking about N.S., I have to say they rented the apartment upstairs, but they would come only on the weekend. They said were still working in Jacksonville.

The second Sunday that we were working at the Hotel, we came back home to find that our apartment had been burglarized. They took the VCR, and some jewelry and I think they were looking for money. We called the police who made a report, but nothing happened. It is still a mystery for us, who came inside the apartment. Of course, we couldn't judge anybody, yes?

But after that incident Napoleao came back, I think, only one more time. First he said they would come back to Gainesville, and some time later he called me saying he would be moving back to Chicago, and always saying he would pay us.

But to this day we have not received one cent, and I promise if before I finish my book we receive some money, of course, I would open a special part in my book and say "Listen, Napoleao (who was not the Bonaparte), paid me and made his word right!!!!!" But I can say I feel sorry for him, he is a disoriented person, lost in the world.

After our place was burglarized, we did not feel safe living in the same house. Of course we needed to wait some time to have money in hand. We did not have credit history in Tampa, and didn't know anybody.

Then we moved to Morrison Court. It was a better area, with more security. After the burglary we knew we were living in a low security area in Tampa, in East Tampa.

We did not stay long at that second apartment either, because we did not like the cleanness of the building. There were a lot of roaches and it was too small. We stayed there only around 2 or 3 months looking for another place to move. At that time we heard that my nephew Mauro was coming during his vacation to visit us. From there we moved to the Coachwood Apartments, on Bayshore Boulevard where we stayed until we moved from Florida in March of 1991.

We continued to work at the Holiday Inn Hotel. The work was hard and made us tired but we were afraid to leave. We were still paying for the car, by now it was our second car in Florida, an 83 Mustang, named MUSTA. The SAFIRENTO was too old and had so many problems, like starting, we were scared it could leave us walking some day.

One other thing made us stay at the Hotel. The next December we would need to apply for our permanent residence in the USA, and someone had said me that for the application we needed to include our work place. I got so upset because when we applied for the green card (permanent residence), nothing was asked about the job, only our personal information, like address and so on.

In August, Mauro came to visit us during his vacation for two weeks. He liked it a lot, but for us it was not an easy time. Money was very tight, for example to invite him for dinner, but he rented a car and traveled, went to Disney World, and the east coast. After Mauro left, Celia Nascimento came to visit us too. She came very quickly to Tampa and we felt great to see our friends and relatives again.

In November, Neida's nephew, Sergio, who was living in Massachusetts, came to visit us too. It was great to have him for a couple days. It was almost his time to come back for good to Brazil. After that we needed to stay in Tampa, working hard at the Hotel and waiting now for Zulmira, my sister, to come to visit us. Since September she had been waiting for the airplane tickets. Finally in January she came.

At the same time, September or October, we heard from M.D., who was living in Framingham, MA. She was married and pregnant; the baby was expected in December. She asked us to move to Framingham and live with them. They would rent a two bedroom apartment, and we would divide the expense with them. Neida and I accepted that offer, because really we wanted to move from Florida. We were still thinking of moving back to Chicago where we had a lot of friends, but then we were glad to have this invitation to go to Massachusetts and live there with the them.

L.M. from Chicago comes to visit us and we stayed together for the New Year. It was very nice for us have Luiz with us, because it was he who first welcomed us when we arrived in America.

Finally Zulmira arrived on January 15, 1991 in Orlando and we went to pick her up. It is hard to describe how Neida and I were so amazingly happy. Not only happy it was like a feelings of LIBERTY. Zulmira came to our house and we were free to leave Florida after her visit.

She stayed with us only 3 weeks; it was not a lot time but was amazingly great for us. We tried to go out with her a lot and she bought things for her 2 granddaughter's We went to St.Petersburg beach, Clearwater, and to the Busch Gardens.

She loved to go with us for lunch, to every fast food place here, and she was glad to go for dinner, when we went to celebrate Neida's birthday on February 10. Abdul, Neida's boyfriend, went with us too (the Egyptian one). It was funny because she didn't know almost any English, and Abdul did not speak Portuguese, then? Neida and I all the time had to translate for them both.

At that time, I could say I loved to find humor about many things that were happening, because keeping good humor was better to keep me healthy and everyone around me happy too. For example, since we moved to the last apartment, at Bayshore Boulevard, every day when we went to work we needed to cross a street named EUCLID. And all the time, or better say every time it reminded me of an old TV program from Brazil, when a man sent errands for the EUCLIDES, and I would imitate his funny voice.

I need to say about my noise that always I made with my stuffed bears. The first one was named Ted.

Unfortunately I left him in Chicago with Elisangela, Gentil's daughter. In Tampa, as soon as possible, Neida gave me a new one FRED (Frederick), with whom I talked, slept (always hugged him), and made new clothes for him. Oh Lord after 50 years old, getting to live that way is really something, everyone must be thinking. But it is better to live that way instead of sniffing around.

After Zulmira went back to Brazil it was only a question of time, waiting for our 1 year anniversary of working at the hotel, and handing in our resignations and getting the 2 weeks' vacation.

T hen, for the second time we sold everything we had, but we did not make good money. It was less than in Chicago and we sold the car, too. On March 23rd we left Florida and went to our 3rd state in America. We went to Massachusetts.

MASSACHUSETTS

Sometimes, I like to go back in time and make some analysis. When we left our Country the first idea was to come here, make some money and go back. But day by day we changed our minds.

I can say the 2 years and 5 months that I lived in Chicago was a good time, I enjoyed the experience with the Gembick family and I made money to go and visit my mother who was starting to have a problem with her eyes, losing her vision.

But after returning from Brazil I had a hard time finding a job. Finally I was able to earn good money again as a babysitter, and then appeared the great "dreaming idea" to move to Florida.

After that difficult time, it was like a transition for us. We never felt we were established in Florida. Then we moved to Massachusetts, on the day we completed 3 years and 6 months in America. We were anxious but at the same time with a lot of hope that better days would come for us.

In Massachusetts we came to share an apartment with a friend of mine and her husband. We lived with them only 5 months and one week.

We decided to travel by train again; it was cheap and convenient for us. Of course, it took 30 hours to get to Framingham, MA, and we had some setbacks too, during our travels.

Neida's boyfriend, Abdul, brought us to the train station. His car was small so he needed to take us in 2 trips. The second time, they arrived late, believe that? Neida is originally from Minas Gerais, the state where the people never miss the train, and she almost missed the train!

Amtrak did not accept one of our bags, it was too heavy. They asked what was inside, I said: VCR's tapes! Then they said no, that luggage we must carry inside the train with us.

We left Tampa at the correct time. Until New York we had a great trip, the worst part was from New York to Framingham.

First we needed to wait more than 2 hours at the New York train Station. We were worried about how many homeless people were at the Station and asking for cigarettes from Neida (Neida was a smoker at that time).

Finally we departed, but the man who helped us carry the bags put us on the last car of the train, and always I was saying "We will go to Framingham."

The train was so full (it was a Sunday evening). When they came to check the ticket, he said that at New Haven we needed to move to the first 3 cars, because only those 3 cars would go to Framingham.

My Lord! At New Haaven station, I thought I would die! To carry that heavy luggage! But we won. Worse was that at that stage in between New York and Framingham (5 hours), there was no restaurant car on the train, and at the small bar there was nothing to buy, and we were hungry.

We arrived in Framingham at 7.30 PM on March 24th. I called M.D. on the phone (she told me before they lived not far from the train station). Her husband was there in less than 10 minutes.

All of our bags went to Boston, because Framingham is a small station. We knew that would happen. We were so happy to get home after more than 30 hours. We were really hungry, since we had no restaurant car on the last train. They offered us only coffee and cake (bolo), can you imagine? In the bedroom, where Neida and I were going to sleep, we found nothing! Only the empty and clean room, with closet and carpet?

M.D. knew our bags were going to go to Boston. We had almost nothing in hand. Could you imagine that? She did not ask me if I wanted her to buy or borrow a mattress to sleep on. And in the end she got us something like comforter to put under our bodies to sleep. It was a great welcome we had at her house. It was awful, I would say unbelievable.

Always I said "It is OK." But to myself I said "We'll see how long we can stay with them!" From our conversation on the phone, I knew they were not happy in that apartment in Framingham. She told me it was noisy in the building. Neida and I did not hear that much noise and it understandable for us, because there we were paying $650.00 for the rent of the 2 bed rooms. At Natick we would pay $700.00 for the 2 bed rooms; the only improvement was that it would have 2 bathrooms, one for the master bed room (theirs) and another for me and Neida, and of course for visitors, too.

We arrived in Framingham, like I said the hope of finding better jobs. But without a car in Framingham or Natick, it would be impossible, because there was no public transportation. In Framingham we were not far from downtown.

We needed to buy a car. M.D.'s husband at that time had two jobs. He was a hard worker without time to help us; it was completely comprehensive for us. He tried to give us that help. We saw a car, but it was too expensive for us.

Then on Thursday of the 2nd week, I decided to look by myself, and in the newspaper I saw an advertisement, called the number and a young Brazilian man answered and he recognized my accent. I bought the car. It was a little dark, really it was night time when we saw it. It was a Ford Granada 1980, like a big bathtub. I called it NUMBER 5, because it was my 5th car in America. I kept it for only about 3 months, but it helped to find a job for both of us.

M.D. had a friend who was working at a nursing Home. Her name was Vera. Finally I spoke with her by phone and she encouraged us to go Saint Patrick's Manor and fill out an application for the Nurse's aid position. She said she would go there and talk to the Personnel Department about us. We went there on April 10th. But we continued filling out applications at other places. We wanted work. We went to 2 hotels, McDonald's, a cleaning company, and Neida started working at the Dunkin Donuts in Framingham. We started to be worried, because we came from Florida with little money in hand.

Then Neida started working in Upton, as a companion for an old lady. I called again to the Personnel Department at S. Patrick's Manor, and got an appointment on April 25th. The next day I started 3 days training and then started working.

After the training I started working part time, 20 hours a week, 3 to 7 PM. everything was new for me, because I never had in my life taken care of the elderly. I learned how to give all the personal care: bed, bath, and feeding. At first I was a little scared but I really liked working with the elderly. I felt they needed care and love at the end of their lives.

When I start I was working at one Unit (floor) only with female residents there. It was a little difficult to adapt, but it was fast. I worked part time only one month and a half, and then I got full time with 40 hours a week, 3 to 11 PM. In June I completed the 75 hours training and took the state test, and I received my certification.

At that time Neida was still working in Upton, taking care of the old lady there. Neida lived there during the week and came home only on weekends, and sometimes only on Sundays. Of course she continued to pay the rent. Then started the big divergence between us and M.D. and her husband> I was paying 300 dollars per month, including food, and Neida who was away almost 6 days a week was paying 250 dollars. That was the beginning. But Neida was really was not feeling OK at her job in Upton. Something was not going well for her and she was not happy. Then on July 8th, before I started work, I stopped at the Personnel Office at the Nursing Home, and talked about Neida. She had applied on the same day as I had. They called her for an interview and at the next day she started her 3 days training and started working full time, 40 hours a week on the 3rd shift, 11 PM to 7 AM.

I forgot to say that car "number five" was starting to give us a lot of trouble. It was leaking oil and it was an old car to be fixed. So we bought a Hyundai Excel 87, but that car was not automatic. Neida needed to take a class to practice and learn to drive a standard car. It was not a big problem for her, except that she needed to sleep in the morning, after the night shift, right? M.D. had a little girl at that time 7 months old, and was babysitting for another child the same age.

We sat down with them to try to talk it out. It was getting impossible for us to continue living with them, we were spending 350 dollars a months and not feeling comfortable, because Neida now needed to rest in the morning. And with 400 dollars we could rent a small apartment of our own.

So, we left the apartment in Natick on August 30th, 1991. Unfortunately they completely cut the relationship with us, because they wanted us to pay one more month of rent. We did not really understand that.

I felt really bad, because I knew M.D. since she was 15 years old, when she first moved to Rio de Janeiro from her hometown of Minas Gerais. She come to work and study at a school where I was living at that time I was a nun. And after that time, when I was director at a school at Duque de Caxias, in 1986, she worked there and had been preparing to come to America.

When before I came I called her, and she did not open her house to me, and now that she was interested for us to share the expenses she called and invited me? We came but stayed only 5 months and in the end she completely cut the friendship. Then no reason for a friendship? That's too bad, but this is life!

Then, we started life in our 3rd place to live in America. At that time we moved to Framingham, on Edgell Road, it was great because it was very close to St Patrick's Manor, and we paid only $400.00. It was a one bedroom. I continued to work 3 to 11 PM, and Neida worked the night shift. The only difficulty was that, with only one car, I needed to pick Neida up at 7.00 AM. I asked to change my shift to work the same hours as Neida. I was having some trouble sleeping at night, maybe because I was alone home and needed to be there at 7:00 am to pick her up? I really don't know.

Then on December 1, 1991 after 7 months on the evening shift I started working the night shift. I liked it. The routine was completely different, but it was not complicated to adjust. I continue working on the same floor, E2, which was easy because I knew all the residents.

Like I said, when I started work at the Nursing Home, everything was new for me, because until that time I worked all my life taking care of children. But I got along very easily. Of course at first I had a hard time with some chores, especially because at that first unit almost all the residents were bed bound, and to do transfer from bed to wheelchair and vice versa was not easy. But I learned and loved my elderly new friends at that I usually called "my ladies."

I remember every time I entered the room of Sarah C., I used to sing in my Language "Adeus Sarita" and I think she recognized my voice (I always sing out of tune - "desafinada") and she always looked at me and tried to communicate back.

And I remember when I was working the night shift, when I entered Mary's P. room and said "hi," she answered me in the same tone as my "hi," and always said "I like that," like she wanted to say "I like you."

Then I started to prepare to go to Brazil for the 2nd time to visit my mother and stay with her for Mother's Day. I would have 2 weeks' paid vacation and 2 weeks without pay. It would be great for me to rest a little, visit my family and come back with a lot of power to work and make money, may be to try to come back to Brazil for good.

But this life has so many roads, and at the end we feel the reality that we don't know anything about tomorrow.

Everything was all set for my trip, with the tickets in hand, all the shopping done. I remember at the end of January I had my physical exam and my first mammogram on April 7th. The week after the mammogram my Primary Doctor called me and said I needed to have another mammogram, because one area in my right breast was not clear. I had it done again at Natick's Hospital and an Ultrasound too, and they detected a small lump.

My Doctor called me and said I have to have a lumpectomy done, to take the lump for a biopsy. She sent me to a surgeon who wanted to do the procedure the next week. I was scared to death, having surgery done less than one month after the 1st mammogram.

The next Saturday, before I went to work, I stopped at S.Patrick's Manor to talk with the person responsible for the schedule. I explained to her my situation: I have 2 weeks vacation, and 2 weeks without pay approved. She completely understood, and said to me not to worry about my time to go to Brazil, but first to take care of myself.

She gave me the name of a great surgeon, very experienced in lumpectomy. She also explained the right way to request a second opinion. I got the approval from my Health Insurance. After seeing Doctor Fam I decided to book the surgery, because I felt more comfortable with her than with the first doctor.

I change my time off from work to begin May 24th. The Surgery was on May 26th. I stayed at home one week before going to Brazil.

Everything was done correctly and easily. Before the surgery I went to the Radiology Center. They put a needle with a bulb lamp in my breast, and then they brought me to the Surgical Day Care. When I said good bye toNeida she was more nervous than I was.

In the surgery room, I saw Dr.Fam. She was so cheerful for me. They put in the IV and I fell asleep in seconds. When I woke up she was at my side telling me everything was fine and she would tell my daughter (Neida) about my surgery.

I got home around 2:00PM. I followed all the instructions and precautions they gave me and I did not feel pain at all. After 2 days I received the biopsy result and thank God the lump was benign. I stayed home one week before I traveled to Brazil, and Neida was on vacation too.

Finally on June 3rd I left for Brazil. I went to Boston and then New York. I went by Transbrasil which I did not like because I had to stop at Brasilia and S.Paulo. I arrived In Rio de Janeiro at 2:30 AM. Zulmira, Walter and Janete were waiting for me.

This second visit was completely different from the first one; of course the First is always the First. I stayed at Urca, at Zulmira's house, because my mother's house was full. My brother Ivinho was living there with his family, and I was recuperating from my surgery. It was great. I could enjoy Tianna and Mariana, Zulmira's granddaughters who were 4 years old and adorable girls.

At that time I had some more grandchildren, Camila, one year old, Diva's Grand daughter, Rodrigo, Paulo's grandson, Andre's son, and Ivo Neto's second child, Fernanda. The only one I did not see was Gustavo, Ismail's grandson.

I stayed there this time for only 18 days. I had the opportunity to participate some days at the Forum Global, part of ECO 92, The Earth Summit, which was happening while I was there.

I went to Copacabana, on my uncle Iris' birthday and met a big part of my family. I went to the Instituto Isabel to visit some old friends of mine, Sister Ines, the oldest one at the Congregation at 95 years old, Sr.Deliria, Sr Rita and Luzinete.

But? Life is like that, on June 21st I was back in the USA, and now at that time with different feelings about my personal life. Of course I was more stabilized. Neida was working and I came back to my regular Job. Only about my mother I was worried. I felt her worse (depressed?). Her life seems very sad because of her health situation, she almost lost her vision, and her house was full of people.

More and more I could analyze her life and mine and I really came to the conclusion that, if at this time if I decided come back to live in Brazil, I would not solve her problem or mine either.

Then? Once more I decided to continue to live my life like I was in a BOAT, always rowing the oar in the same direction. Without that, the boat could sink. Am I right? The most things important now was to live and keep my life in God's hands.

MY WORK WITH THE ELDERLY

Then, since I come to Massachusetts, it was like I have change my mind about my job, because instead of children, I start working at Nursing Home and I really enjoy work with elderly and giving to them not only the care they need but, my love and comprehension at the end of theirs lives, and I can say I always work these way.

Saint Patrick's Manor was the first facility where I had worked, and had experience to work at the 3 shifts they have. First it was 3 to 11 PM shift, at that time it was only around 7 months, then it was 11Pm to 7 Am, when I made great friends, and work for 2 and ½ year, but at the end I start to get very tired and I change again. That time I tried work at 7 Am to 3 Pm. It was good too, but may be, for me it wasn't that great, special about the rush hours, of appointments with doctors, hair dressing, Chapel, and so on. Then after that I come back at the 3 to 11 shift, and never changed until I get my Retirement.

MY PCA WORK

At July/1992, I was still working at the 3rd shift when I decided do a PCA work, and my first client was M.L. I made a good relationship with her. She was almost my age, handicapped and she was living in Natick, at one building for seniors and she could have by the Independent Living one PCA help.

Usual I was going to help her at the evening, most of the time 2 to 5 PM or something around that, she was very flexible and it was very easy for me. And when I say it was a great relationship, it means I could trust her about my book, about the real goal of nit. She gave me a lot help, I already said about that at the Introduction of the book.

I work for M.L. until July/95, but after that I keep in touch with her and always giving some help for her. When my sister Zulmira come to visit me in Massachusetts, she went with me to visit her, and since that M.L. keep in touch with my sister by sending Cards and letters.

Other good things that happening at that time, was that I met one wonderful lady, who was volunteer and friend of her, A.H. It was great for me have so nice friend, and she help me and my friend Neida, when we had some kind of trouble with the Immigration of Tampa, Fl., because we had change the address, now to Massachusetts, and they say they couldn't send our green card to Boston. And then A.H. was friend of one Framingham representative and we receive our Green Card is Boston, and it was fast and easy.

See? It was amazed the friendship connection, that I had made in all my life.

At 1995, I took care of M.E. every other weekend, when I go to her house in Wellesley, and stay with her, when the other girl was having her time off. She was a great experience too for me, I made that around 3 or m4 months, but I get tired because I did not have a weekend off.

At S. Patrick's Manor, I made private for M.G., she was a Resident there, and I was going some evenings there and she was a great friendly too, it was from October/95 to May/96.

At January and February/97 I went to Weston to help R.G., she was the mother of one friend mine, and giving some help and company at the evening time, it was before the time I had to go to Brazil, because my mother was very sick.

THE HOME HEALTH AID

At February 1995, I took a 20 hours training at Natick VNA, and get my Home Health Aid Certification, and then I start working for agency doing the Home Health aid, and the first one was Interim Health Care Inc.

I work for Interim from May/95 to September/95, when I had a car accident, it was not that bad but I stay without car for couple weeks. I really enjoy doing that, and I took care of one lady at Wellesley, I was going there every morning.

TLC was other Agency that I worked from September/96 to Janyary/97, and I come back again from September to November/98, and at that time the agency was sending me where place they need help, really I did not have my own schedule, I like any way, because the people were waiting for us to come and help them.

PARMENTER HEALTH SERVICE

At Parmenter, in Wayland, I work from April/97 to May/98. I work full time. And there I have my regular schedule, most of the time. I can say I really enjoy, special because I had opportunity to work with HOSPICE.

When I moved to Shrewsbury, I decided to quit, because it was far away from me, most of my clients were far for me.

MY WORK AT ASSISTED LIVING

I start work at Heritage in Framingham at September/96, it was at night shift and then they have a open position at 7-3 shift. I work only at that shift for 2 months, because it was at one Alzheimer Unit, and it was very hard for me and I resigned.

And after that, January/97 until April/97 I was only working ON CALL at St. Patrick's Manor, and for TLC and some privates. Finally I get the full time job at Parmenter Health Care, that I said above, where I really enjoyed.

And after 5 months I start again work at St Patrick's Manor, now working at the Convent, every other week end, it was from November/97 to nov/98, and at November/98 I start complete my 32 hours, working again at the Nursing home(St. Patrick's Manor)and at the weekend at the Convent. And at September/99 I start working full time, only at the Convent. And at February /2004 I get my retirement.

Really since the year 2003 I was thinking to apply for my retirement. But I decided to keep working, it was not at the right time for that. But definitely when I start 2004, I start to get very tired and Then I decided to apply for my retirement, at Feb/5th I went to the Social security office at Framingham, and I made the date March/1st/2004.

After that it was simple, I talk with the Nurse, my boss, and at the Personnel department, it was very well done, and February/27th was my last day working at the Nursing Home , of course I would miss my elderly people, and the really make for me a wonderful party, to say good bye.

MY MOVING AT MASSACHUSETTS AND MY TRIPS TO BRAZIL

It is funny, how many times I had moved in Massachusetts, seems like a have blood of gipsy.

I said already, after we live around 5 months with M.D. family, in Natick, we move to one apart at the Edgel road, it was august/91.

Then at 1994 I decided to go Brazil, using one Law about Family Absent Leaving, and I could stay out for 12 weeks, because my Mother was sick and need me.

And really at that time she was not doing so well and it would be nice if I could spend with her some more time.

And most of the time at that my visit to Brazil I stay at her house, and of course some times at Urca too, special because Denise was pregnant of her 2nd child, and I offer myself be the Godmother, because at the same day the three Zulmira's grand children get the baptism, Tianna and Mariana they were 6th years old and Gabriela was born on October/1st.

Of course it was great time for me to spend some more time with my family and special with my mother, she was starting to be so fragile, but I took her out with me for a couple times. Once we went to Copacabana to Visit my Aunt Isa and I remember other time we went to Zulmira's house, she went to see her great grand child Gabriela.

I just come back to America at November and the life keeps going on, like always.

And I was talking about the Place we had live at Framingham, it was a small place, but it was not that expensive at that time, then we stay there until September/95 when we bought a condominium Town House at Bishop Drive, in Framingham.

It was amazed easy the process to buy a property in the USA,, because we had good Credit, not a good money.

It was at 1996 , me and my mother at my 55th Birthday Celebration (05/05/96).

At 1996 I decided to go to visit my mommy and celebrate with her my birthday, because it seems to me be a special one, I would be 55th years old, and I was born at 05/05, then? I felt special way to be there at her sided really she was so happy with me and the celebration I made.

I order one "FEIJOADA", my family was almost there, it make me feel so great, and really t was my last birth day I spent at her side, and since I was a little girl I could feel how this day, May/05 was important for her.

At that time I had only my Aunt Cecy and Uncle Iris alive(my father's siblings), and they came at my party and all my sisters and brothers were there too.

I came back to America and always I kept in touch about my mother's health situation, never stop keeping calling my sisters., doesn't matter for me how expensive it would be so many phone's call.

Then when my sister Zulmira starting say me that my mother was refusing eat, and starting have some episodes of talking with the death people, like my father and Paulo, my brother who passed away, I decided to fly to Brazil (taking the Airplane, of course) almost at the next day.

At that time she was not having yet treatment with a Gerontologist, she was seeing only a Clinical Doctor at Nossa Senhora da Gloria Hospital.

The first day she starting to have the same time, of be out of her and talking with dead people (and she was starting be some aggressive too) we brought her at the Emergency Room at the Marcilio Dias Hospital (it was the main Naval hospital at Rio de Janeiro), and get her hospitalized for couples week.

Finally she came back home, and she completely recuperated at that situation, and of course I had to come back to my life at America.

Then return about the place we were living, I could repeat,

We were very happy there, but for many reasons we lived there only until April/98, when we decided to sell the apart. We were thinking to buy another one, but it was not may be the right time for that. Then we move to Shrewsbury, where we rent one apartment at one Condominium. It was nice place to live, but some far away from Wayland, and I had to quit my job at Parmenter Health Service.

That time we were living there, we had 2 visits from Brazil. First was my cousin Marisa, she stay one months with us, and I remember we celebrate her Birthday with a special dinner and so on, it was September/98.

At May/ 1998 I decided go to Brazil go again to Brazil and spend with my mother the Mother's day. Always it was easy for me to find a reason to go to Brazil and spend with her n some time. And it was funny, that most of the time I prefer stay at Urca, because always her house with full, with my brother Ivinho and family living there, but almost every single day I took the bus or metro and stay with her, because really she was not doing that good , getting fragile all the time.

And at that time I remember I decided to bring with me to America Angela Maria, because her twin sister, Maria Angela was living already at Chicago. Since she move to Chicago I made contact with them (they were living at one Orphanage at Uberaba-MG, when I was there 1969-1972)

I was so glad I took the opportunity to bring Angela Maria with me, and from Boston she went almost directly to Chicago.

And, next January of 1999 my brother Ismail came with Maria Angela (his wife) and Maria Beatriz(her sister). They stay only around 10 days, but we had a very good time together.

Life? Say Yes to Life

Then at the end of one year we move to Marlborough, we rent one house at Lincoln St., "The YELLOW HOUSE", it was not a easy time for us, because the Landlord, was not a easy person to deal, we had problem, that we never had before, but we survive (like always).

At July/27th/1999 I went to Brazil again, it was my 8th Visit. I was there for 35 days, and it was the most agitated trip I had.

At July 4th, I heard from my sister Zulmira that my mother had been hospitalized , she was having some kind of clots, at her left leg, then in one week I decided to go there, first to be with my mother and second I want to meet one person, which one I was talking at the Internet, since april/28th.

My mother left the Hospital at July/21st and at July/28th I was arriving there.

About this man, F.Y., I could say it was a nice dream I had, and I paid ($$$) for that. I was completely involved for that news at my life:" Some body saying me he was in LOVE with me, but now I can say how I was blind, I was not listening anybody, and I was "In love".

He was starting to say me something, but I couldn't, or better, I was not interested to know nothing. Could you imagine, he put my name at one street at CaboFrio? It was a proof of love, believe?

And of course I went to Brazil first to see my mother, and then to meet this person and at the 35 days I was there, for 12 days I was in contact with him, and at the others one I always I communicate or by Phone, or Chat, or e mail, I was always looking for a Computer to get on line, and communicate with him, reading his messages. I could say it was nice for me to know him; he seems a nice person, very kind with me.

But, when I come back to my place, at America, I could analize every line he wrote to me, and every inter line too, at every chat we had, then I realize he had something, he use to say, need to say in my language "Oculto pelas estrategias", this means he had something nothing clear (Oculto) by the strategies, and I prefer don't talk about that, here at my book. Then I completed stopped any contact with him, only keeping with me the good time I had either at the Luxor Hotel, at Leme or at the COCHICHO DO XANDICO, at Cabo Frio.

When I was at Cabo Frio, at the second time,, I took the opportunity to visit at Arraial do Cabo, my cousin Sonia Maria and her mother, Aunt Cecy, and really was a nice time we had together.

Other good thing I made was going to Guaxupe, where my brother Ismail was living. I met Ismail at S.Paulo, at Claudio's place.

In Guaxupe I stay only 3 days, but it was good time I had, I met a lot of my family there, and for some hours I went to Pocos de Caldas too.

I remember at that time I had opportunity to visit my cousin, Dr. Sylvio Ribeiro do Valle, who is a doctor and son of my uncle Mario(my mother's brother).Then I could talk with him and my brother about my book, and by the first time I talk with somebody about what I heard from my Mother, when I was 12th years old, when she was asking about the possibility that my paralyzed face be consequence of one injection she had taken. Unfortunately the name of that injection is gone from my mind. I kept that name for long time. And really my cousin agree about that, the possibility I have this parestesy about the Injection.

Then from that date I start to talk openly with some member of family about that, reality of my life, and don't ask me why I had kept that inside myself. First it was Denise and Janete, Zulmira's daughter, and lately Claudio, Ismail's son.

But please keep in mind Marta, never talk and ask about that subject, but at the other side she always felt extremely protect by God.

And I need to write here one simple phrase I read, don't remember where, and who wrote:

"What we are is God's gift to us…

What we become is our gift to GOD…."

I kept this words in my mind, because God let me come at this world, and I think I am trying to give Him back my life and been good around me.

Then, I was almost coming back to USA, and F.Y. came to say good bye for me, come to Maria da Graca house, and met my sister Diva too. And he went with me at Zulmira's house at Urca, went for lunch at Garota da Urca, and it was the end of one faze of my life.

At that house, the YELLOW HOUSE, we had some visitor from Brazil, Neida's sister Lucilia and her daughter Vivia and almost at the same time Fabio, Neida's nephew came too.

And then we decided to buy again, I look at the Internet and found some places in Marlborough and I call T.C. and he return my call, it was interesting he speaks Portuguese too, his family originally from Azores, and he was a nice friendly person.

We bought the apartment at the Wayside condominium, and move there at May/1st/2000.

And at that time I had everything all set for my trip to Brazil, I want stay with my mother at Mother's Day and when I come back Roberto and Lucilia, Neida's siblings they came with me, Roberto to try his life in America and Lucilia only for a couple months, and went back to Brazil.

And about my trip to Brazil it was good for me to spend some more time with my mommy, and really was her last Mother's Day, and believe or not she almost alone with one of that lady who was Companion of her, and I went to buy food for our lunch, and only later at the evening she receives visits from my other siblings.

I was very happy because one friend mine, from the Internet, he lives at Juiz de Fora, MG, he had asked me my mother's telephone numbers and he sent to her, my mother, in the morning, one cute and great Phone Message, it was so grateful for me.

At that time I had opportunity to meet some others friends that I had made at the internet.

First I went to Olaria where I met Maria and her sister Nydia, it was so nice and I slept there one night with them. And I went to Niteroi to meet Anita and Martha, who came from Sao Paulo, and it was amazed funny and I slept there too one night.

I think it was natural my feeling when I came back to America, it was like I was saying good bye for her because she was not in a good health, so fragile she was and her skin so broken, it was like a soft paper. At that time she was still walking, not very good, but was going to eat at the dinning room, and to the bathroom, always with one person at her side.

But in July, when she had the next Doctor's appointment, her situation was very worse; she was not walking any more and start the bed sore in her body. And she was kept for a while , under the Home Care, by the Hospital Naval N. Senhora da Gloria.

In October she had to be hospitalized at one Tuesday and at the next day I was flying to N York and to Rio de Janeiro. I went to the Hospital and I was on her side for five days. Adequate medical care the possible attention that could be given was what she was getting. There was, however, no improvement. I knew somewhere deep inside me but was afraid to say, to disclose it even to myself that she was dying, that she was not to survive the present hospitalization, she become almost a skeleton, with her little body, almost a texture of the unfinished doll and reminded me of those dolls she use to prepare for us, all brothers and sisters when we were children.

But I had some satisfaction That I could make it and could see her during her last days, she was nearing the death, and the show must go on, I told myself once more. I could stay there only for five days, because I had to come back, there was an urgency. There was one appointment with INS, and I was required to be present in person to give my fingerprint, needed in regarding to my Citizenship.

But I came back carrying with me a load of uncertain moments, an uneasiness and restlessness. While back in MA, I had all become ears , all attentive even during the sleep, unconsciously to telephone… probably waiting for the unpleasant news. And then there was a call from sister after two days, disclosing that unpleasant news. My mother had died.

Of course my life had change a lot after that, but? We need to keep going, right?

It was in Massachusetts, 2001, at my Naturalization ceremony with Neida my best friend.

About the year 2001, I have to say something special that happening, first was the Naturalization Ceremony of me and Neida, it was at 03/8th/2001, it was really a wonderful time. It was a Westin Hotel at Boston., it was held by the 32nd Northeast Conference on The social Studies. And after the Ceremony we had some reception for us. And Roberto, Neida's brother was living with us and went and took goods pictures.

But? Life is made not with good things, then at March/25th a fire happening at the building where we were living, at Wayside Condominium.

It was at 4.30 am, Sunday, we had to evacuate the building, nobody get hurt, and believe or not the fire had been stop(contained) at the next wall of our apartment. See how amazed blessing we were, and no one drop of water we had. It was not an easy time it was not, and many consequences we had to deal.

We need to be out the building, of course we had to go at one Red Cross shelter, at one local school, I need to say so great was the American Red Cross, how quickly they made that. But we did not had to sleep there, because we went to friends houses, 2 nights at Luciana and Jesiel and other 2 nights at Georginette's houses. And after that we had another blessing, T.C., the person which one we bought the apartment, almost one year before, he gave us a key of one of his house at Hudson, where we could live the time we need for the reconstruction of the building. Then we move to Hudson and live there for 13 months.

This year, 2001, I went to Brazil September/27th two weeks after the incident of 09/11. It was some kind of scary, and everything was ok. I fly to Miami, and had to wait there 8 hours for my International flight. I really went to Brazil at that time, for stay and commemorate Gabriela's Birthday. She was waiting for that, and it was a nice time we had.

At this time I went to S.Paulo to meet my friend Martha Maria and it was so nice time we spend together, and I slept there, and other friend mine, from Taubate, Myrna came to meet me. And after that I made a day trip to Juiz de Fora, MG, to meet my friend Ademar and his wife and son, I took a Bus and it was a very easy, and great time I hade. And I went to have lunch with my Friend Jacy and his wife, at their apart at Tijuca.

See? Really I had opportunity to made, at the Internet, nice friends, and some of them are still wonderful to me, until today.

And after I come back to America, after 13 months we were living at Hudson, we move back to our apartment at the Wayside Condominium, it was at May/2002.

Of course our Brazilians friends, most of them originally from Crisciuma, Santa Catarina, helped us again.

It is really amazed how they are glad to help us to move. And, finally, before that moving, we made a barbecue for them, because they from south of Brazil, and they love "Churrasco".

In June/2002 I went to Chicago, I had been invited to go to the wedding of Lella, the older girl that I was baby sitter in Chicago.

And really it was a great time I had. She was so beautiful, and Nika too, who was her maid.

And at the Reception I sit at the Family' table, side with her Grand mother.

And of course I had opportunity to visit other old friends mine, and I stay with Maria Angela e Angela Maria houses, remember the twins from Uberaba?

At november/2002, I went to Brazil, for the first time together with Neida, we feel great for that, it was only for two weeks. I went to Rio de Janeiro and Neida go to Divinopolis, and I went to Divinopolis for only a couples days, because it was the Confirmation of Tainara, Neida's nice and she invite me to be her God mother.

It was nice that I have opportunity to be with Neida's family again, because before I come to America, I became Godmother of Brunna Maria, Neida's grand niece; it was at April/1987.

Now I need talk a little bit about my pet. At January/23rd/2003 I get a cute bird, a Cockatiel. We named him LUCKY. When he came to us he was I think 7 weeks old, little tine one. And with me and Neida, around him, he grew up so smart and beautiful bird.

He speaks two languages, sings (whisttle) the American Banner, and Brazilian Hine too, and a lot others one. And it is funny how he knows about our routine, the breakfast time, the hour to pour the coffee and get the sugar in…and at Lunch time is a Toast time for him too.

He most the time wake me up every morning, scream loud (he must know I have hearing problem): MARTA BABY…

And when I am away from home is unbelievable how he express he is sad. And when he is Happy how he knows to laugh. He is completely attracted with any piece of paper or any cartoon box.

Really Lucky gave for us a great companionship.

When I start the year 2003, I was convinced myself, and saying to everybody, that I was not plain go to my Country at that year. But at the day of my Birthday, Zulmira and her family had called me at the phone and really I couldn't resist when I heard the voice of Tianna and Mariana, then? I decided to go. Of course the first thinking would be the Fifteenth Years Party for both of them.

It was my 3rd trip to Brazil after my mother died and how I felt her close to me, it was really a short trip too, only 6 days there. But at those 6 days I did not stop, my time was for shopping, dinner, lunches at many places, I know my family miss me there.

When I come back I was so tired, but so tired, I couldn't sleep until Miami. But I was happy myself, happy had been there and happy be back to USA where my life is now.

Like I said before, I get my retirement at March/01st/2004, it was great for me, but? At that time, it was not an easy time, because my brother Ivinho, was very ill, he had a Gastro Cancer, it start at his mouth and kept at his Esophagus. It had start around 3 years before, and he start to get worse and worse, had made quimio, everything they could.

The day before my last day working(it was Feb/27th- My mother's Birthday), I talked with him at the phone, his voice was with a terrible sound, and he seems to me he was confident they would get a surgery, because they had put a Feeding tube, for him recuperate weight for the procedure.

And he could stay home only for a couple days, then he get Hospitalized again. And now they send him to a Hospital, special for treatment for clients at the Terminal stage of cancer.

Then I was home, happy about my retirement, but my head, was so far, my thinking was about my brother so suffer he was Then, of course like always I made I decided go to Brazil.

I was glad I went, because I saw him twice, and he passed away at my 3rd day there, it was like the pain stopped for him, but I felt empty inside. It was amazed for me thinking that he was living at my mother place, she died at year 2000. My brother's wife, Elba died at 2002 and now he died at 2004.

But, two days after the Funeral I had to come back to America, I can say it was the worse flight I had had in all my life. I left Rio, need stop at S.Paulo and change the airplane, I start get some cold symptoms, believe that I get sleep and miss the diner? Almost at 3 00 am, I wake up and ask for some food…finally I arrived safe. And after that trip I get sick twice with bronchitis, and had to get some antibiotics.

If you ask me what reason for that? it was hard to answer, but I really had in my mind need to look for a part time job, then? What to do? It was not easy time. Then, I remember , it was at May, one night I couldn't sleep(very unusual for me) , and I was reading one weekly local magazine with advertisement of the local communities and I saw, one advertisement about Babysitter BEFORE AND AFTER SCHOOL, in Marlborough. I called next day, left message and the mother call me back, they live I can say almost at the corner of me.

Then I make one interview with the family. And it was for two little girls at the same age of my first 2 girls in Chicago, and then I made commitment with the family and start working at the last week of August.

See? How my life is amazed protected by God?

At my country my work was with children, came to America and kept that way, when in Chicago. When I moved to Massachusetts I had work with the elderly for almost 13 years and now I am back working with children again?

And one other thing very interesting. I grew up, living at Professor Lafayette Cortes Street and I study the High School at Lafayette Institute and now the family live at Lafayette Drive, at Marlborough.

Around one week before I start this part time job, I had one idea, to buy the apartment 102(constructed for my father). It was like to solve one familiar matter, like if I put my parent's property in a better shape, and of course I would regularized the situation of the apartment 101(from Maria da Graca).

But after one week of negotiation, and talking with my siblings at the phone or by the Internet, I decided to stop that decision, and I sent to them this paragraph at E mail:

I HAD A DREAM…

Really I had a dream to preserve my parent's property, buying the apartment 102, and regularized the situation of the bedrooms of apartment 101.

But, for many many reasons, I decided to stop, before I start this process:

1st: because I am starting my baby sitter working, and of course, no possibility I have to go to my Country for that, during the school period.

2nd: because I am at one time of complete dedication to finish and publish my book.

Then, please forget , at the moment, what I said at the phone or at the Internet. And of course I will include this paragraph in my book.

(I sent by internet)

Then, that's Marta, now trying very hard to finish the book that I propose to write, and remember who first gave that idea was the mother of the two girls in Chicago, and now I am here taking care of the 2 beautiful little girls again.

It was at Christmas 2004, with my two little ones that I am babysitting (2004/2005)

I can say, that I am proud to be myself like I am. And my book never means to be only a protest or something like that against the abortion. No, my book is a commemoration of LIFE.

I am here, I am alive, and I can say honestly, and modesty at side, that I lived my life with a lot of love that I received and love that I certainly gave for everybody around me, at first my family, then the children that I took care, at so many schools and orphanages, in my Country. Then the elderly that for almost 13 years I cared, respected and loved.

And sure at this time how I remember my Mother. I came to live here at USA, but at so many times I went there, to spend time with her. Any thing happening was a reason for me to go there, for example when I was going to commemorate my 55th years I went there, and now, she is not there any more, but I am plain to publish my book at 05/05/2005. I hope it could happen and make my mother and father happy where they are.

And listen, I am completely sure they are at GLORY of God, and looking after me.

Printed in the United States
by Baker & Taylor Publisher Services